Welcome to Milan, Bergamo and the Lakes

1

Spire of the Duomo
© MaxBaumann/iStockphoto.com

Getting to Milan

BY PLANE

Milano Linate Airport

www.milanolinate-airport.com -
📞 02 232 323 - 7 km east of Milan.
By bus – For downtown Milan: lines **73**
(every 10min, 5:50am-12:54am - 40-min
journey - 1.50 €) or **X73** (Mon.-Fri. - every
20min, 7:10am-7:50pm - 25-min journey -
1.50 €); to Piazza San Babila (M1). For the
Stazione Centrale (M2 and M3): the **Starfly**
line (www.airportbusexpress.it - every
30min, 5:30am-10pm - 30-min journey
- 5 €) and **Airbus Linate-Centrale**
(every 30min, 6:30am-11:30pm, 30-min
journey - 5 €).
By taxi – Allow 20/25 €.

Milano Malpensa

www.milanomalpensa-airport.com -
📞 02 232 323 - 50km north-west of
Milan. Two terminals: **T1** for international
and domestic flights, **T2** for the low-cost
airlines.
By bus – For the Stazione Centrale:
Malpensa Shuttle (www.malpensashuttle.
it), or **Malpensa Bus Express** (www.stie.it)
or **Terravision** (www.terravision.eu), dep.
from T1 and T2 every 20/60min - 50-min
journey - 10 €. The Malpensa Shuttle bus
also runs between airports Malpensa and
Milano Linate.
By train – **Malpensa Express** (www.
malpensaexpress.it - every 30min,
6am-12am - 30-min journey - 13 € - dep.
from T1 and T2 for stations Milan Cadorna
(M1), Garibaldi (M2 and M5) and Centrale
(M2 and M3).
By taxi – The fixed fare between Malpensa
and Milan is 90 €.

Bergamo Orio Al Serio Airport

www.milanbergamoairport.it - 📞 035
326 323 - 45km east of Milan.

By bus – For Stazione Centrale: **Orio
Shuttle** (www.orioshuttle.com - every
30min, 3:50am-11:40pm - 50-min.
journey - 5 €); the **Terravision** bus
(www.terravision.eu - every 30min,
4am-1pm - 50-min. journey - 5 €) and the
Autostradale bus (www.autostradale.it -
every 30min, 7:45am-1pm - 1-hr journey
- 5 €).
To get to Bergamo: **Airport Bus** (www.atb.
bergamo.it - every 20min, 6am-12:25am -
15-min. journey - 2.10 €).

BY TRAIN

From France – Daily TGV connections
from Paris (Gare de Lyon) for Milan, 7hrs.
📞 3635 - www.voyages-sncf.com.
From Switzerland – Daily connections
departing from Zurich (4 hrs) and Geneva
(4 hrs) for Milan - fr.rail.cc.
From Milan's Stazione Centrale or Stazione
Garibaldi, departures every hour for
Bergamo (journey time 50-70 mins) -
www.trenitalia.com. To the stations
Milano Centrale (M2 and M3) or Garibaldi
(M2 and M5).

BY BUS

Eurolines – 📞 0892 89 90 91 - www.
eurolines.fr. Departing from Paris and
numerous cities in the provinces, regular
lines to Milan. Journey time Paris-Milan,
Lampugnano bus station (M1): 15 hrs.

> ### Milan metro
> **Open:** 6am-12:30am.
> **Prices:** 1 journey (valid 90min) 1.50 €; 24-hr
> pass 4.50 € or 48hrs 8.25 €.
> **Website:** www.atm-mi.it.
> ⏷ Map on reverse of detachable map.

Stazione Centrale
© LeeYiuTung/iStockphoto.com

Unmissable

Our picks for must-see sites

Duomo★★★
Map: E5 - 🕭 p. 14

Novecento Museum★★
Map: E5 - 🕭 p. 16

Sforza Castle★★★
Map: CD4 - 🕭 p. 20

Basilica of St. Ambrose★★★
Map: C5 - 🕭 p. 46

The Last Supper★★★
Map: B4 - 🕭 p. 49

4

Pinacoteca di Brera★★★
Map: E4 - ♿ p. 28

San Lorenzo Maggiore★★
Map: D6 - ♿ p. 41

Bergamo★★★
♿ p. 59

The Borromean Islands★★★
♿ p. 68

Bellagio★★★
♿ p. 80

Our top picks

💜 **The Terraces of the Duomo.** Perched 70m above the ground. Take a stroll among the pinnacles, buttresses, gargoyles and saints; look out for the statue with Mussolini's face on it, sculpted during restoration work in the 1920s. Enjoy stunning views of the city on all sides. *See p. 16*.

💜 **A night at La Scala.** Although getting a ticket to this opera house can often seem like mission impossible (except for seats that cost over 100 €), check anyway to see what's on and find out when tickets go on sale *(www.teatroallascala.org)*. You could be in for an unforgettable evening. *See p. 18*.

💜 **Villa Necchi Campiglio.** This rationalist gem by Piero Portaluppi is tucked away in a quiet part of town, known as the Quadrilateral of Silence, in stark contrast to the far more animated Quadrilatero d'Oro (rectangle of gold). Come see what life was like for an upper-class Milanese family in the 1930s. *See p. 26*.

💜 **Triennale Design Museum.** Situated in the heart of Parco Sempione, this radiant space celebrates one of the things at which Milan excels: design. Round off your visit with a bite to eat at Triennale Design Café. *See p. 21*.

💜 **Early morning in Brera.** The nightlife, the fortune-tellers and bric-a-brac stalls, the *dolce vita* Milanese... the Brera district is well-known for all of that. If you really want to feel its essence, though, take a stroll here in the early morning to experience its village-like atmosphere and enjoy the coolness of the little courtyards adorned with flowers and the silence of the alleyways before they wake up for the day ahead. *See p. 28*.

💜 **Aperitivo in Navigli.** Sip a wine spritzer with your feet dangling in the water or, better yet, while taking

6

Triennale Design Museum

© claudiodivizia/iStockphoto.com

© meseberg/iStockphoto.com

Isola del Garda

a boat trip around the city's most picturesque district. **&** *See p. 44.*

💙 **The frescoes of Bernardino Luini at San Maurizio.** This church may seem unassuming on the outside, but inside you'll find frescoes reminiscent of the Sistine Chapel, painted in the 1530s by Bernardino Luini, a pupil of Da Vinci. **&** *See p. 47.*

💙 **Piazza Gae Aulenti.** Step into the future at this square dominated by the iconic Torre Unicredit, the tallest building in Italy. **&** *See p. 51.*

💙 **Isola di San Giulio.** Floating in the middle of little Lake Orta, this delightful islet, home to a Roman basilica, is an enchanting place.

Let the signs guide the way and contemplate the stillness around you. **&** *See p. 73.*

💙 **Villa del Balbianello.** This beautiful 18th century residence, used as a set in *Star Wars* and *Casino Royale*, rises high among cedars and cypress trees. Like a sentinel, its magnificent loggia keeps watch over the two shores of Lake Como. **&** *See p. 78.*

💙 **Isola del Garda.** On arrival, you'll be given a warm welcome by the Borghese-Cavazza family, who will tell you all about their island, their palace and their family's heritage. A delightful place. **&** *See p. 85.*

Milan in 3 days

DAY 1

▶*Morning*
A visit to the complex formed by the **Duomo**★★★ (*p. 14*), leaving time to go up to the panoramic **terraces**★★★. Stop for something sweet at **Marchesi** (*p. 100*), then visit the **Museo del Novecento**★★ (*p. 16*).

▶*Lunchtime*
Cross the **Galleria Vittorio Emanuele**★★★ (*p. 18*) until you reach the **Piazza della Scala** (*p. 18*) where a traditional *panzerotto* (similar to a calzone) from **Luini** (*p. 90*) is perfect for a quick and easy lunch. For a more sophisticated gastronomic experience, head to the third floor of the Mercato del Duomo, where you'll find **Spazio Milano,** run by the pupils of chef Niko Romito (p. 90).

▶*Afternoon*
Head down the elegant Via Manzoni and explore the **Quadrilatero della Moda**★ (*p. 23*). If you're keen on more fine art, you can choose between the **Gallerie d'Italia**★★ (*p. 19*), the **Museo Poldi Pezzoli**★★ (*p. 22*)

8

© Yoko Aziz/age fotostock

Evening aperitif in Porta Nuova

and the remarkable **Museo Bagatti Valsecchi★★** (p. 24). If you prefer to continue wandering around the city, head down **Corso Venezia★** (p. 24) until you reach **Giardini Montanelli★** (p. 27).

▶*Evening*

When it comes to seeing Milan by night, the best places to be are the Brera and Porta Nuova districts. Enjoy an aperitif at one of the many bars on **Corso Garibaldi** (p. 31) or at **Bulgari** (p. 102), haunt of the fashionistas, before having dinner in the area.

DAY 2

▶*Morning*

Visit **Sforza Castle★★★** (p. 20) where you can see Michelangelo's moving ***Rondanini Pietà★★★***. Stroll across **Parco Sempione** to the **Torre Branca**, from the top of which there's a magnificent **view★★** (p. 21).

▶*Lunchtime*

Go for a quick lunch at **Triennale Design Café** (p. 101).

▶*Afternoon*

Visit the **Triennale Design Museum★** (p. 21), then head to Corso Magenta and **Santa Maria delle Grazie★★** (p. 49). To see Leonardo da Vinci's ***The Last Supper★★★*** (p. 49), consider booking in advance. If you have time, visit the church of **San Maurizio★★** (p. 47) and/or the Basilica of **St. Ambrose★★★** (p. 46).

▶*Evening*

Explore old Milan in all its intimacy and enjoy a traditional dinner at **Trattoria Milanese** (p. 93), with its can't-miss *risotto allo zafferano*.

DAY 3

▶*Morning*

Visit one of the two big museums in Milan: the **Pinacoteca di Brera★★★** (p. 28) or the **Pinacoteca Ambrosiana★★★** (p. 32). Head to the Ticinese district and walk along **Corso di Porta Ticinese,** stopping off at the **San Lorenzo Basilica★★** (p. 41) and **Portinari Chapel★★** (p. 42) at the Basilica of Sant'Eustorgio.

▶*Lunchtime*

Have lunch at one of the many eateries in the lively **Corso di Porta Ticinese** (p. 42).

▶*Afternoon*

In Via Tortona, the HQ of Milanese fashion, visit **MUDEC★** (p. 45), the Museum of Cultures, inside a former factory. Make your way to the **Navigli★** for a boat trip (p. 44) or a stroll beside the canals.

▶*Evening*

Aperitivo on the Navigli. For dinner, head to **Solari district** (p. 45).

Days 4 & 5: Bergamo and the lakes region

You can spend a whole day in Bergamo, and then move on to the romantic setting of the lakes. Choose between the western shore of Lake Maggiore, Lake Como or the western shore of Lake Garda.

9

Visit Milan, Bergamo and the Lakes

11

Tram passing in front of Teatro alla Scala
© Leonid Andronov/iStockphoto.com

Milan today

Dynamic and cosmopolitan
The economic and financial capital of Italy, Milan is also a global center for fashion, design and good taste. Its cosmopolitan aspect is coming ever more sharply into focus thanks to urban transformations involving countless world-renowned architects —Sir Norman Foster, Massimiliano Fuksas, Zaha Hadid, the Libeskind studio, Cesar Pelli & Associates, Stefano Boeri—who have regenerated former industrial wastelands and shaped the face of the Milan of tomorrow. This is a city full of energy, where the miracle of creativity is a permanent fixture. Modern, needless to say. A hub for the country's industrial, artistic, financial and political avant-garde. A metropolis that is always open to change, thanks to an incredible capacity for innovation.

The search for beauty
Métropole restée à taille humaine, Milan is not a museum-city like Rome, but the richness of its **historic legacy**, something visitors often have no inkling of, will delight art-lovers. An aesthetic city above all else, with its Duomo but also its elegant church Santa Maria delle Grazie, balanced and distinguished, as though the architect Bramante had specially embellished this ensemble so as to better complement the famous *The Last Supper* by Leonardo da Vinci, a statue of whom stands across from La Scala. The Lombard capital is also home to the Brera and Ambrosiana galleries, which have two of the most extensive collections in the world.

The cult of visual beauty is not confined to the walls of the museums, though. **Decorative art**, while not accessible to everyone, has its global center in Milan. *Milano Design Week* (in the spring), which also hosts the Furniture Fair, is an unmissable international event for design, in all its many forms.

Milan is, of course, **one of the capitals of fashion**, something it celebrates on the catwalk during the famous *Fashion Weeks*. The countless showrooms in the Quadrilatero della Moda reveal to visitors brands Gucci, Prada, Giorgio Armani and Versace, magical names that evoke a world of elegance and invention.

Milanese hipsterism
Milan is an elegant beauty, like its inhabitants, always dressed up to the nines. There's an intense buzz at its trendy cafés and bars around **happy hour** time, and you can feel it in the countless footpaths and shopping streets in the historic center too. From the intimate Brera district to the on-point and glittering 'Golden rectangle of fashion', Milan is a must-see destination for anyone who really wants to understand modern Italy and sample a *dolce vita* that is very much alive and well.

The gods of the soccer stadium
The city's two teams, AC Milan and Inter, put on a show that at

12

times makes even the calmest *tifosi* (supporters) go wild. Soccer is perhaps the key prerogative for a city constantly in motion, and the San Siro stadium is almost as sacred as the Madonnina.

District after district

With no river, few instantly recognizable monuments, and a flat skyline, Milan offers few landmarks aside from the brand new skyscrapers in the Porta Nuova and CityLife districts. The **historic center**, around the Duomo, is ringed by boulevards built on the former canals (the **Cerchia dei Navigli**)—now filled in, though they may one day be restored—which formed the boundary of the Roman and medieval city. The **Cerchia dei Bastioni**, a series of boulevards built at the site of the Spanish walls, marks the city's expansion until the 19C and forms a second concentric circle. This 'hypercenter' is bordered to the west by the former **Fiera**—now the **CityLife** district—and to the east by the **Città Studi** (a university area with science faculties), both characterized by long, often tree-lined residential avenues and flanked by beautiful Liberty-style buildings. The **northern districts** contains several points of interest, such as **Isola** and **Porta Nuova**, the Cimitero monumentale and the Stazione Centrale.

As for the heart of the city, its various component parts open on either side of the axis linking the Duomo

© Nikada/iStockphoto.com

Versace store on via Montenapoleone

13

to Castello Sforzesco. To the north of the castle are the most upmarket areas, particularly the ultra-famous **Quadrilatero de la moda** and the very select and trendy **Brera**. To the south, sample the unique charms of other areas brimming with history, such as **old Milan**, the **former canals** district, or those of the **Navigli**, **Magenta** and **Sant'Ambrogio**.

This patchwork of districts is a source of countless rich and diverse opportunities for discovery.

Duomo to Castello Sforzesco★★★

This is the beating heart of Milan! The route from the Duomo, a majestic cathedral, to the imposing Castello Sforzesco—fully pedestrianized and always packed—is lined with alluring shopfronts and the beautiful façades of old buildings, revealing the commercial and business-oriented soul of the city.

▶**Getting there:** Ⓜ Duomo (M1 and M3), Cairoli and Cordusio (M1), Lanza (M2) and Cadorna (M1 and M2). *Map of the area p. 17. Pull-out map BE 3-5.*
▶**Tip:** Allow one full day.

PIAZZA DUOMO★★

This immense square—one of the largest in Italy at 17,000 m²—was designed by Giuseppe Mengoni and completed in 1873. It allows visitors to get a sense of the vastness of the cathedral, which dominates the esplanade. Adorned with an **equestrian statue of Vittorio Emanuele II** at its center, the square is lined with buildings from various eras, the most recent one being the Palazzo dell'Arengario, home to the Museo del Novecento (Pietro Portaluppi, 1928). On the west side, opposite the Duomo, note the unusual palm trees, planted in 2017, a cause of controversy, as they were deemed a little too exotic by the Milanese.

DUOMO★★★

Construction of this impressive masterpiece of the flamboyant Gothic style, colossal yet boasting a lightness of touch, began in 1396 at the initiative of Gian Galeazzo Visconti and continued into the 15C and 16C, involving artists and engineers from Italy, France and Germany. Begun in the 17C, the major work on the façade was completed under Napoleon Iˢᵗ, but the doors were not finished until 1950. With some 135 spires and more than 3,200 statues, the white marble exterior is breathtaking. Walk around the edifice to admire the magnificent proportions of the chevet, dominated by the large spire; the spire is 108 m tall, in the middle of the transept, and is topped with a golden statue of the Virgin, the **Madonnina**, which is cherished by the Milanese.

⊘ The 7ᵗʰ floor of the **La Rinascente department store** (& *see 'Where to drink' p. 100 and 'Where to eat', p. 116*) gives visitors a close-up view of the architectural and sculptural details of the rooftops.
Visit – ℘ 02 72 02 33 75 - *www.duomomilano.it - 8am-7pm - cathedral and museum 3 €; Duomo Pass A (terraces by elevator, cathedral, archaeological zone – baptistery and*

14

Piazza del Duomo and Galleria Vittorio Emanuele II

Santa Tecla – and museum) 16 €; Duomo Pass B (like Duomo Pass A but without the elevator) 12 € ; cathedral, archaeological zone and museum 7 €. No shorts or sleeveless tops. The security checks can lead to long lines.

In contrast with the exterior, the very somber interior creates a sense of austerity and heaviness. The dimensions are enormous: the cathedral is 148m long and 88m wide across the transept. The five Gothic naves, punctuated by 52 columns, are adorned with magnificent stained glass windows, the oldest of which date back to the 15C and 16C.

The transept on the right houses the mausoleum of Gian Giacomo Medici by Leone Leoni (16C) and an intriguing statue of Saint Bartholomew, the martyr who was flayed alive, by Marco d'Agrate. Has beautiful, sumptuous furnishings, particularly the Baroque stalls and master-altar attributed to Tibaldi.

In the **crypt**, among the **treasure**, you can see the silver urn containing the relics of Saint Charles Borromeo, archbishop of Milan until his death in 1584, and some masterpieces in silverwork and ivory associated with veneration. You can continue your visit by heading to the archaeological zone, which incorporates the Paleochristian **baptistry** and the 4C **Santa Tecla** basilica.

Terraces★★★
9am-7pm - 13 € by elevator, 9 € on foot (165 steps).
Among the buttresses and turrets and the hundreds of statues—some of which date back to the restoration in 1920 (boxers fighting and a portrait of Mussolini)—the terraces offer a superb panorama of the city and, in fair weather, of the Alps too.

MUSEO DEL DUOMO★★

Ⓜ *Duomo - entrance under the arcades of the royal palace, on the left - ℘ 02 86 03 58 - www.duomomilano.it - every day except Wed 10am-6pm - 3 € - collect an audio-guide at the entrance (6 €).*
This museum, which got a makeover in 2013, races the history of the cathedral in its architectural, artistic, cultural, economic and social aspects. The visitor route, which follows a red line that works chronologically and thematically, enables visitors to discover a magnificent ivory diptych from the 5C, the silver **evangeliary of Aribert★** (11C.), the splendid **Crucifix of Aribert★★** (1040), the original versions of the statues (the only way you can see them up-close), the stained glass windows (1540-1550) of Corrado de Mochis, some beautiful tapestries (note the sublime *The Deposition*, woven in 1520 in Brussels) and, at the end, the astonishing wooden **model★** of the Duomo (16-19C).
San Gottardo in Corte – Once you've visited the room with the stained glass windows, a small detour leads to this former ducal chapel (1366), containing a superb octagonal Gothic **campanile★** that can be glimpsed

from the courtyard. Inside, admire a beautiful *Crucifixion* in a style inspired by Giotto *(rear wall on the left)* and, in the manse, the sarcophagus of Azzone Visconti (1339).

PALAZZO REALE

The former royal palace was built in the 18C by **Giuseppe Piermarini** and incorporates numerous Gothic traces of the former ducal palace. The large **salle des Cariatides** is the most important of the surviving rooms, although it was severely damaged during the bombing raids in 1943. The palace often serves as the setting for major art exhibitions in the city.

MUSEO DEL NOVECENTO★★

Via Marconi, 1 - Ⓜ Duomo - Palazzo dell'Arengario - ℘ 02 88 44 40 61 - www.museodelnovecento.org - 9:30am-7:30pm (Thurs and Sat 10:30pm), Mon 12:30pm-7:30pm - 5 € or Tourist MuseumCard (♿ see p. 128).
The Arengario, built in the 1930s to a design by Portaluppi, Muzio, Magistretti and Griffini, houses this museum dedicated to the arts of the 20C. The famous painting *Quarto Stato* by Pellizza da Volpedo is the work that greets you when you visit the collection. Painted in 1901, it depicts, with stunningly expressive power, a group of workers and peasants heading towards a future that is full of hope. The collections are displayed in chronological order, following the major movements of the 20C, up until Arte Povera, as illustrated

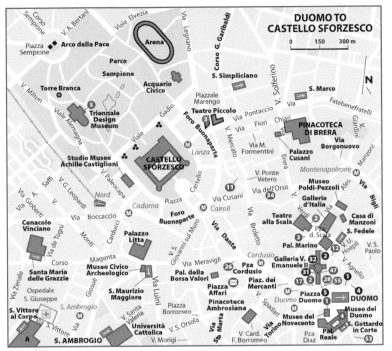

DUOMO TO CASTELLO SFORZESCO

0   150   300 m

N

Corso Sempione
V. A. Bertani
Viale Elvezia
Via Legnano
Via G. Garibaldi
Piazza Sempione
◆◆ Arco della Pace
Arena
Corso G. Garibaldi
Parco Sempione
V. Solferino
S. Simpliciano
S. Marco
Fatebenefratelli
Acquario Civico
Piazzale Marengo
Via Pontaccio
Torre Branca
Triennale Design Museum ⑤
V. Milton
Viale Alemagna
Gadio
Foro Buonaparte
Teatro Piccolo ③
V. Mercato
Via Fiori Chiari
PINACOTECA DI BRERA
Via Borgonuovo
V. Giardini
Via Manzoni
Studio Museo Achille Castiglioni
V. Paleocapa
Viale
Lanza
V. M. Formentini
Palazzo Cusani
Montenapoleone
CASTELLO SFORZESCO
Via Brera
Ales.
Via Bigli
Nord
Saffi
V. G. Leopardi
Cadorna Ⓜ
Castello
V. Ponte Vetero
Museo Poldi-Pezzoli
Via A.
Via Gioberti
V
Via Boccaccio
Piazza Cairoli Ⓜ
Via dell'Orso ㉞
Gallerie d'Italia
Via A.
V. U. Hoepli
Foro Buonaparte
Via Cusani
Teatro alla Scala
Verdi
Casa di Manzoni
Cenacolo Vinciano
Via de Togni
Monti
Carducci
Via Dante
Via Broletto
Pza d. Scala
S. Fedele
V. S. Paolo
Corso Magenta
Palazzo Litta
V. S. Giovanni sul Muro
Pal. Marino
③
⑫
V. Agnello
Santa Maria delle Grazie
Museo Civico Archeologico
Via Meravigli
Cordusio
Galleria V. Emanuele II ㉜
⑰ ㉛
㉘ ㊴
⑤ ㊵
Via Zenale
Ospedale S. Giuseppe
S. Maurizio Maggiore
Pal. della Borsa Valori
Pza Cordusio Ⓜ
㉖
Piaz. dei Mercanti
Piazza Duomo Ⓜ
DUOMO ①
DUOMO
S. Vittore al Corpo
Via S. Vittore
S. Ambrogio
S. Santa Valeria
Piazza Affari
Pinacoteca Ambrosiana
Spadari
Duomo
Museo del Novecento
Museo del Duomo ④
Via S. Marta
Università Cattolica
V.S. Orsola
V. Card. F. Borromeo
Via Torino
Pza Diaz
Pal. Reale
S. Gottardo in Corte
㊽
Ⓐ S. AMBROGIO
V. Morigi

WHERE TO EAT	WHERE TO DRINK		
Emilia e Carlo............⑪	Pasticceria Marchesi....㊼	Sky Terrace Hotel Milano Scala............㊴	La Rinascente.............①
Jade Café...................㊼	Café Trussardi............③	Triennale Design Café..⑤	Versace....................㉜
Luini Panzerotti.........⑫	Camparino in Galleria..②	SHOPPING	NIGHTLIFE
Mercato del Duomo (Il)....㉘	Duomo 21 Terrace.......⑰	Borsalino..................②	Piccolo Teatro............③
Ristorante Giacomo Arengario...............①	Galleria Meravigli Bistrot...................㉖	Feltrinelli..................⑤	Teatro alla Scala.........②
Spazio Milano...........㊵	Giacomo Caffè...........④	Furla.......................④	Museo Nazionale Leonardo da Vinci.......Ⓐ
		Prada......................㉛	

by their most significant artists: De Chirico, Sironi, Morandi, Fontana, Manzoni. At the heart of the museum, the magnificent **salle des Colonnes**

contains the biggest collection of works of **Futurism★★** in the world: **Boccioni**, Balla, Carrà (*voir p. 143*). From the room dedicated to Lucio

Fontana, there is a wonderful **view★★** of the cathedral.

GALLERIA VITTORIO EMANUELE II★★★

🅼 *Duomo.*
Milan's iconic arcade, constructed in 1877 to a design by Giuseppe Mengoni, forms an enormous cross whose glass and steel vaulted ceiling that stands 50m tall and houses high-end stores, cafés and restaurants. Its recent refurbishment brought a fresh sparkle to the magnificent decorations. On the 6th floor of the building, where you'll find the Marchesi patisserie (🅰 *see p. 100*), **Milano Osservatorio** is a new space forming part of the **Fondazone Prada** (🅰 *see p. 40*), dedicated to photography exhibitions. It offers an unusual perspective on the glazed ceilings and windows of the gallery. *🖉 02 56 66 26 11 - www.fondazione prada.org - 2pm-8pm, w/end 10am-8pm - 10€ (combined ticket with the Fondazione Prada).*
A little farther on you will see groups of people clustered around one of the mosaics decorating the floor: it is said that if you put your heel on the testicles of the bull in this mosaic—the bull of the house of Savoy—it will bring you luck. At the end you can make out the **Piazza della Scala**.

TEATRO ALLA SCALA★★

Piazza della Scala/Via Filodrammatici, 2 - 🅼 Duomo - 🖉 02 88 791 or 02 72 00 37 44 - www. teatroallascala.org.
The most famous opera house in the world, built by **Piermarini** between

1776 and 1778, has a surprisingly simplistic exterior that belies the magnificence of the auditorium itself. The theatrical season begins on 7 December, the feast day of **St. Ambroise**, with a big gala evening. A costly renovation orchestrated by the architect **Mario Botta** in 2004 enabled the corridors to be extended, giving the building's profile a new shape that veers more towards the original than the aesthetically pleasing. A fresh round of enlargement works, also undertaken by Mario Botta, is on the agenda for 2019. The splendid horseshoe-shaped auditorium is remarkably large: with its six floors of boxes it can seat up to 3,600 spectators. The acoustics here are exceptional, even when you're seated up in the highest seats.
Museo teatrale alla Scala★ – *Piazza della Scala - 🖉 02 88 79 74 73 - www. teatroallascala.org - 9am-5:30pm - closed during rehearsals - 9 €.*
The museum houses a large amount of memorabilia associated with major figures from the lyric and dramatic arts from all ages. You can access one of the boxes, and take a look at the auditorium, directly from the museum.

PALAZZO MARINO

Piazza della Scala, 2 - 🅼 Duomo or Montenapoleone - free visits by appointment via 🖉 02 88 45 66 17 or DSCOM.VisitePalazzoMarino@comune. milano.it.
Across from La Scala, this palace, built by Alessi in the 16C for the Genoese banker Tommaso Marino, has been home to the **town hall** since 1861.

It was the birthplace of Marianna de Leyva, the granddaughter of Tommaso Marino, who was to form the inspiration for the character of the nun Monza, in Manzoni's *The Betrothed*. The façade opening onto the Piazza della Scala dates from 1892, whereas that of the Piazza San Fedele (*& p. 22*) corresponds to the building's original entrance. Inside, the palace has some beautifully decorated rooms.

GALLERIE D'ITALIA★★

Piazza della Scala, 6 - Ⓜ Duomo or Montenapoleone - ✆ 800 16 76 19 - www.gallerieditalia.com - every day except Mon 9:30am-7:30pm (Thurs 10:30pm) - 5 €. Allow 1 hr 30 mins.
The Milanese parts of the banking group Intesa San Paolo's extensive art collection are dedicated to the Italian art of the 19-20C and are housed in magnificent palaces. In the sumptuous **setting★** of the historic building of the **Banca Commerciale Italiana** (1911) works by some of the great names of Italian art in the 20C are on display (Fontana, Guttuso, Afro, Burri, Capogrossi, Consagra, Vedova, Baj, Schifano, etc.). The bank's rooms and former cashiers' windows are well worth seeing in their own right. The **Palazzo Anguissola★**, a breathtaking neo-classical palace, contains the wonderful bas-reliefs of **Canova** and works (mostly from Lombardy) from the various artistic movements of the 19th century: romanticism, historicism linked to Risorgimento, landscapes, genre painting, divisionism and symbolism. Room 14, dedicated to the Navigli of old, evokes the network of canals that once criss-crossed Milan, making it look like a 'water city' (*& see info box on p. 140*).

PIAZZA DEI MERCANTI★

Ⓜ *Duomo or Cordusio.*
'Merchants' Square', quiet and picturesque, is located in the heart of medieval Milan, and has been miraculously well preserved. The **Palazzo dei Giureconsulti**, a Renaissance style palace (1564), features an unusual square tower and a statue of St. Ambrose teaching. The **Palazzo della Ragione** (or **Broletto Nuovo**), built in the 13C and enlarged in the 18C, contains an equestrian statue, tucked away in a corner, of the Podestat Oldrado da Tresseno, a Romanesque work produced by the **Antelami**. It is used for photography exhibitions (*www. palazzodellaragionefotografia.it*). The other palaces in the square feature Gothic loggias and arcades, with no real consistency of style but a great deal of harmony.

PIAZZA CORDUSIO & VIA DANTE

Ⓜ *Cordusio or Cairoli.*
A lively intersection, the **Piazza Cordusio** is dominated by the imposing and eclectic Palazzo delle Assicurazioni Generali (1899). From the Via Cordusio, head to Piazza Edison, then walk down Via della Posta to **Piazza Affari**. The buildings here, in Milan's answer to Wall Street, are enormous. The **Borsa Valori**, or Palazzo Mezzanotte, adorned with an imposing travertine marble façade,

was erected in 1931 on the site of a Roman theater, traces of which still exist under the ground. In the middle of the square is the cheeky statue **L.O.V.E.** (Libertà, Odio, Vendetta, Eternità, 2010), a provocative work by the artist Maurizio Cattelan.

Leading away from Piazza Cordusio is **Via Dante**, a pedestrianized street, with Castello Sforzesco as its backdrop. A shopper's paradise, this wide inroad, which dates from the 1890s, is lined with elegant neo-Renaissance buildings.

FORO BUONAPARTE

Ⓜ *Cairoli.*

The façades stretching out in a semi-circle across from the château constitute the **Foro Buonaparte**, whose grandiose layout stems from a project by Napoleon Ist, not built until the end of the 19C.

Studio Museo Achille Castiglioni – *Piazza Castello, 27 -* Ⓜ *Cadorna - ℰ 02 80 53 606 - www.fondazioneachille castiglioni.it - guided visits by appointment Tue-Fri at 10am, 11am and 12pm, and also at 6:30pm, 7:30pm and 8:30pm Thursdays - 10 €.*

On the left-hand side of Piazza Castello, the workshop of the great Milanese designer (1918-2002) offers visitors the chance to see his creations.

CASTELLO SFORZESCO★★★

Ⓜ *Cairoli - ℰ 02 88 46 37 03 - https:// milanocastello.it - 7am-6pm (7:30pm in the summer) - free.*

Built from the 1450s onwards by the Viscontis and later home to the Dukes

of Milan (the Sforzas), this square, brick fortress, encircled by deep moats, boasts impressive dimensions (with sides almost 200m long). The large towers along its façade, which dominate the Piazza Castello, were all restored in the early 20C, except for the square central tower, which was entirely rebuilt. Arranged around two attractive courtyards with refined Renaissance-style arches, the **Cortile Ducale** and the **Cortile della Rocchetta**, the wings of the fortress house some remarkable art collections.

Musei del Castello★★

Ticket office at the back of the Cortile delle Armi, on the right - ℰ 02 88 46 37 03 - 9am-5:30pm - closed Mon - 5 € or Tourist MuseumCard (⚫ see p. 128). Allow 2 hrs 30 mins.

Museo Pietà Rondanini★★★ – *Cortile delle Armi - grd. fl.* One of the treasures of the château's collections, this space, inaugurated in 2015, is a sparingly designed, almost mystical place, dedicated to Michelangelo's last, unfinished masterpiece (1564).

Museo d'Arte antica★★ – *Cortile Ducale - grd. fl.* This museum houses collections of sculptures and weapons in splendid rooms with vaulted ceilings, and paintings adorning the walls; the most beautiful of all are the **Sala delle Asse★**, with frescoes by **Leonardo da Vinci** (1498) depicting an amazing jumble of leaves, and the **Cappella Ducale**. Among the masterpieces, it is worth lingering in front of the imposing **funerary monument of Bernabò Visconti★★** (14C), topped with an equestrian statue of him, and the **statue of a**

reclined **Gaston de Foix**★★ (1517-1522) by Agostino Busti, known as **Bambaia**.
Museo dei Mobili★ – *Cortile Ducale - 1ˢᵗ floor.* This remarkable museum looks back at six centuries of the history of furniture, from the Middle Ages to the present day.
Pinacoteca★ – *Cortile Ducale - 1ˢᵗ floor.* The pinacoteca contains five vast rooms filled with works by the great painters of Northern Italy, from Mantegna to Tiepolo.
Museo degli strumenti musicali★ – *Cortile della Rocchetta - 1ˢᵗ floor.* This museum houses a superb collection of more than **600 musical instruments**.
Museo delle arti decorative – *Cortile della Rocchetta - 1ˢᵗ and 2ⁿᵈ floor.* Contains an interesting exhibition on the decorative arts in Lombardy, from the Middle Ages to the 1960s.
Museo archeologico – *Cortile Ducale - basement.* Includes a section on prehistoric times and one on **Egyptian art**.

PARCO SEMPIONE★

Ⓜ *Lanza or Cadorna.* Milan's most beautiful park is located behind the castle. Here you will discover the Palazzo dell'Arte (👌 *see below*) and the famous **Torre Branca**, a metallic structure built by Gio Ponti and Cesare Chiodi in 1932; from its terrace, perched some 104 meters up, it offers a stunning **panorama**★★ of the metropolitan area (☎ *02 33 14 120 - www.museobranca.it - opening hours vary, check the website - 5 €*). At the northern end of the park, note the **Arco della Pace**★, a triumphal arch erected by Luigi Cagnola (1752-1833) on the orders of Napoleon Iˢᵗ and completed by the Habsburgs. Beyond it is the very wide and imposing **Corso Sempione**, the first section of which is lined with numerous bars and restaurants.
In the east is the **Arena**, designed by Luigi Canonica (1807) and used for concerts and sporting events, and the small but attractive **Acquario Civico**, housed in a magnificent Liberty building constructed for the Milan International, a world's fair held in 1906. *Viale Gadio, 2 - ☎ 02 88 46 57 50 - www.acquariocivicomilano.eu - 9am-5:30pm - closed Mon - 5 € with Tourist MuseumCard* (👌 *see p. 128*).

Triennale Design Museum★
Viale Alemagna, 6 - Ⓜ Cadorna - ☎ 02 72 43 41 - www.triennale designmuseum.it - 10:30am-8:30pm (11pm Thurs) - closed Mon. - 10 €. This museum, by Giovanni Muzio (1893-1982), is a cultural center active in the fields of architecture, urbanism, design and communication. Devoted to Italian design, the museum themed exhibitions that change annually, covering art, industry, and daily life.

21

Quadrilatero della moda and Corso Venezia★★

Milan's most exclusive district is also one of the most beautiful and harmonious parts of the city. Alongside the fabulous luxury displayed in the boutiques of Via Montenapoleone, the area also boasts parks and hidden gardens, tranquil old streets and charming Baroque palaces. The best time to visit is on a weekday or Saturday, when the area comes to life.

▶**Getting there:** Ⓜ Duomo (M1 and M3); Montenapoleone and Turati (M3); San Babila, Palestro and Porta Venezia (M1). 🚊 1, from Via Manzoni to the Giardini Montanelli. ***Map of the area p. 25. Pull-out map EG3-4.***
▶**Tip:** Allow a full day, including the visit to the museums.

22

SAN FEDELE

Ⓜ *Duomo - 7am-2:30pm, 4pm-7pm.*
Intimate **Piazza San Fedele** is home to a monument to Alessandro Manzoni (1883) and the **church** built by Tibaldi in 1569 on the orders of Carlo Borromeo. The interior of the church is a fine example of Milanese baroque. On Via Omenoni is the **Casa degli Omenoni** ('great men'), from the 16C, adorned with eight majestic telamones. The inscription '1722' over the door relates to the old Austrian system of house-numbering, which followed a spiral pattern originating at Palazzo Reale.

CASA DEL MANZONI

Via Morone, 1 - Ⓜ *Duomo - ✆ 02 86 46 04 03 - www.casadelmanzoni.it - 10am-6pm, Sat- 2pm - 6pm -*
closed Sun - Mon - 5 €.
This plush residence where the writer **Alessandro Manzoni** lived for 60 years contains a treasure-trove of memorabilia, photographs, portraits, letters and illustrations from his most famous novel, *The Betrothed*. You can see the great writer's study and bedroom here.

MUSEO POLDI-PEZZOLI★★

Via Manzoni, 12 - Ⓜ *Montenapoleone - ✆ 02 79 48 89 - www.museopoldi pezzoli.it - 10am-6pm - closed Tues - 10 € or Case Museo Card (👌 see p. 128). Allow 1 hr 30 mins.*
Housed in an aristocratic palace dating from the 17C, whose windows overlook a pretty garden, this beautiful museum displays collections of arms, textiles,

© Ludovic Maisant/hemis.fr

Gucci show window, via Montenapoleone, Quadrilatero della Moda

paintings, **clocks★** and bronze pieces. On the 1st floor, the walls are hung with works by the Lombard School (Bergognone, Luini, Foppa, Solario, Boltraffio), **portraits★★** of Luther and his wife by **Lucas Cranach** and, in the Golden Room, the celebrated **Portrait of a Woman★★★** by **Piero del Pollaiolo**, a **Lamentation** and a **Madonna and Child★★** by **Botticelli**, and a mournful **Pieta★** by **Giovanni Bellini**.

In the other rooms are works by Pinturicchio, Palma il Vecchio *(Portrait of a Woman known as The Courtesan)*, Francesco Guardi, Canaletto, Tiepolo, Perugino and Lotto.

QUADRILATERO DELLA MODA★

Ⓜ *Montenapoleone or San Babila.*
The Mecca of Milanese fashion is centered around a rectangular island, combining luxury boutiques and beautiful palaces, and demarcated by Vie Manzoni, Montenapoleone, Sant'Andrea and della Spiga. Why not zigzag from one street to the next: **Via Bigli** to catch a glimpse of sumptuous gardens and courtyards behind the carriage entrances, **Via Montenapoleone** for the priciest window-shopping in Italy, **Via Borgospesso**, **Via della Spiga**, **Via Gesù** and **Via Sant'Andrea**. The great names of international fashion are all

here, and their shop-windows, with their shameless luxury, are in stark contrast to the former palaces and intimate courtyards that house them. To the north-east, admire the 18C façades of **Via Borgonuovo.**

MUSEO BAGATTI VALSECCHI★★

Via Gesù, 5 - Ⓜ Montenapoleone - ℘ 02 /6 00 61 32 - www.museobagatti valsecchi.org - 1pm-5:45pm - closed Mon and in August - 9 € (6 € Wed) or Tourist MuseumCard (Ⓒsee p. 128). Allow 1hr30.

Across from the current residence of the Bagatti Valsecchi family, whose beautiful inner courtyard can be seen, this dwelling was built in the late 19C. by the brothers Fausto and Giuseppe Bagatti Valsecchi, in the Renaissance style. They created a reconstruction of what they imagined an interior from this period to have looked like, combining authentic pieces of furniture with very beautiful copies. The result is extraordinary.

PALAZZO MORANDO - COSTUME MODA IMMAGINE

Via Sant'Andrea, 6 - Ⓜ San Babila or Montenapoleone - ℘ 02 88 44 60 56 - www.costumemodaimmagine.mi.it - 9am-1pm, 2pm-5:30pm - closed Mon - 5 € or Tourist MuseumCard (Ⓒsee p. 128).

A carefully renovated rococo palace recounts the history of the city with the help of sumptuous period costume and a rich collection of paintings of Milan from the 18C and 19C.

CORSO VITTORIO EMANUELE II

Map p. 38. Ⓜ *San Babila or Duomo.* From the rationalist-style **Piazza San Babila** (the church bearing the same name, built in the 11C, was restored in the early 20C), this long and very lively pedestrianized walkway takes you to the Duomo, past a series of boutique stores, cafés and restaurants. Near the start of it, on the right, is the neo-classical church **San Carlo al Corso** (1839), dedicated to Carlo Borromeo.
A short detour takes you to **Piazza Liberty**: the piazza was renovated in 2017 by **Sir Norman Foster** and is home to an underground Apple store (Ⓒsee p. 107).

CORSO VENEZIA★

Ⓜ *San Babila, Palestro, Porta Venezia.* This wide boulevard, one of Milan's most beautiful streets, is lined with imposing palaces in the Baroque, neoclassical and above all **Liberty** styles, the latter having been in vogue in Milan in the early 20C. Note **Palazzo del Seminario Arcivescovile**, at no. 11, **Casa Fontana Silvestri**, from the late 15C (nos.10-14) and **Palazzo Serbelloni** in the neo-classical style (no. 16). Nearby, **Palazzo del Senato** (*Via Senato, 10*), built in the 17C to house a Swiss seminary, has two **courtyards★** lined with loggias with Doric columns. In Via Cappuccini is **Palazzo Berri Meregalli** (no. 8), a striking example of the Liberty style, as is **Palazzo Castiglioni** (Corso Venezia no. 47), completed in 1903 by the architect Sommaruga and the sculptor Bazzaro.

QUADRILATERO DELLA MODA AND CORSO VENEZIA

0   150   300 m

N

25

WHERE TO EAT

Chic and go	34
Il Salumaio di Montenapoleone	20
Joia Kitchen Bistrot	32

WHERE TO DRINK

Bicerin	25
Caruso Fuori Restaurant Bar	28
Emporio Armani Caffè	27

Illy Caffè	32
Lavazza Flagship Store	50
Pasticceria Cova	6
Pasticceria Marchesi	12

SHOPPING

Alessi Flagship Store	12
Aspesi	9
DMagazine	8
ē DePadova	14

Frette	15
Gallo	10
Hoepli	6
Pellini	11
Pirelli Corso Venezia	46

NIGHTLIFE

Armani Privé	14

Villa Reale

© Giovanni Mereghetti/age fotostock

VILLA NECCHI CAMPIGLIO★

Via Mozart, 14 - **Ⓜ** *Palestro - ℘ 02 76 34 01 21 - www.casemuseomilano.it - 10am-6pm - closed Mon and Tue - 10 € or Case Museo Card (♿ see p. 128). Entry to the garden is free. Allow 1 hr.*
Built between 1932 and 1935 on the basis of plans by the Milanese architect **Piero Portaluppi** (1888-1967), the rationalist villa of the Necchi sisters, heirs to the Necchi sewing machine empire, provides an insight into the life of an affluent and cultivated Milanese family.
The exterior gives no indication of the good taste, sobriety and modernity that the ensemble offers: a garden with a heated pool and tennis court,

and, inside, a dumbwaiter, elevator, intercom, wardrobe with automatic lighting. The house contains beautiful furniture and impressive artworks.

GALLERIA D'ARTE MODERNA (GAM)★★

Via Palestro, 16 - **Ⓜ** *Palestro - ℘ 02 88 44 59 47 - www.gam-milano.com - 9am-7:30pm - closed Mon - 5 € or Tourist MuseumCard (♿ see p. 128).*
The museum is housed in **Villa Reale★★**, one of the finest buildings in Milan. Built between 1786 and 1790 by the architect **Leopold Pollack** for Prince Belgioioso, it was the residence of Napoleon Ist during his reign in Italy (1805-1815). The façade overlooking

the park is notable for its sculptures. A pleasant **English garden★** can be found at the rear of the building.
The 19C. collection (the city's largest), and the Vismara collection (20C. Italian and French artists) and Grassi collection (works by Manet, Van Gogh, Gauguin and Cézanne) occupy three floors of the building.
Next door, the **Padiglione d'Arte Contemporanea** (**PAC**) holds exhibitions of contemporary art.
Via Palestro, 14 - ℘ 02 88 44 63 59 - www.pacmilano.it - 9:30am-7:30pm (Thurs 10:30pm) - closed Mon - 8 €.

GIARDINI PUBBLICI INDRO MONTANELLI★

Ⓜ *Palestro.*
These attractive gardens, dedicated to the memory of the great journalist who died in 2001, house the **Planetarium** (*Corso Venezia, 57*) and the **Museo Civico di Storia Naturale★**, a beautiful building dating from 1907 with interesting natural history collections (geology, paleontology and zoology).
Corso Venezia, 55 - ℘ 02 88 46 33 37 - 9am-5:30pm - closed Mon - 5 € or Tourist MuseumCard (& see p. 128).
Cross the park to admire the beautiful 18C façade of **Palazzo Dugnani**.

PORTA VENEZIA★

Ⓜ *Porta Venezia.*
From the neo-classical pavilions of Porta Venezia you can enjoy a wonderful vista of the Corso Buenos Aires (& *see below*). At the corner of Bastioni di Corso Venezia and Corso Venezia is **Casa Rasini**, by Emilio

Lancia and Gio Ponti (1932-35), consisting of a tower and a building made of white marble.
A few paces from here is pretty **Via Malpighi★** (***pull-out map H3***) where you'll see the magnificent Liberty ceramics of **Casa Galimberti** (*at no. 3*) and the cast iron balconies of **Casa Guazzoni** (*at no. 12*).
A short distance away is **Casa-Museo Boschi Di Stefano★**, a house owned by an art-loving couple, who donated to the municipality their tremendous collection of 20C works. Note the room dedicated to Sironi.
*Via G. Jan, 15 - **pull-out map H2** - Ⓜ Lima - ℘ 02 88 46 37 36 - www. fondazioneboschidistefano.it - 10am-6pm - closed Mon - free.*

CORSO BUENOS AIRES

Pull-out map H2-3 - Ⓜ *Porta Venezia, Lima or Loreto.*
The highly commercial and ever-crowded Corso Buenos Aires, which fits over 300 outlets for international chains into its 1.6 km, is a shoppers' paradise for every age and budget.
It leads to **Piazzale Loreto**, famous as the site where the mutilated bodies of Mussolini, Clara Petacci and other Salò Republic bigwigs were put on display at the end of World War Two.

Brera and Corso Garibaldi★★

Brera is Milan's most intimate district. Quiet during the day, it comes alive at night, when the Milanese rub shoulders in the old trattorias, restaurants and new-concept bars. Its 'little village' atmosphere is enhanced by the countless art galleries, antique shops, high-end stores, and the presence of students from the prestigious Fine Arts Academy of Brera, lending the area a non-conformist vibe.

▶**Getting there:** Ⓜ Cairoli and Duomo (M1); Lanza and Moscova (M2).
Area map p. 30. Pull-out map DE2-4.
▶**Tip:** Allow half a day and try to take a stroll here in the early morning, to discover the area at its most charming

OVERVIEW★

The lovely **Via Brera**★ is lined with old palaces, the most imposing of which is **Palazzo Cusani** (*no. 15*), built in the 18th c. On the left are this district's alleyways and little pedestrianized squares (Via Fiori Chiari, Via Madonnina, Via San Carpoforo, Piazza del Carmine); these are among the prettiest in Milan. The terraces, art galleries, fashion stores and antiquarian shops make this an ideal place for a stroll.

PINACOTECA DI BRERA★★★

Via Brera, 28 - Ⓜ Montenapoleone or Lanza - ℘ 02 72 26 32 64 - www. brera.beniculturali.it - 8:30am-7:15pm - closed Mon - 10 € - audio-guide 5 €. Sometimes open at night - check the website. Allow 2hrs 30 mins.
The headquarters of the Academy

of Fine Arts, the Pinacoteca was inaugurated in 1809 by Napoleon I[st], dont une imposante statue en bronze (1811), an imposing bronze statue of whom as *Mars Pacificator,* dating from 1811 and based on a marble sculpture by **Canova**, holds court in the elegant main courtyard. The collection, originally created as material for students to study, then enriched with works taken from churches and monasteries that were closed during the Napoleonic period, is one of the jewels in the crown of Italy's art museums. The project for the **Grande Brera** (still ongoing) will increase the surface area of the pinacoteca by incorporating the **Palazzo Citterio** (*Via Brera, 12*).
The collection is displayed in 38 attractively furnished rooms with coloured partitions which bring out the color palette of the works exhibited. The visitor route is both chronological

© Fine Art Images/age fotostock

Detail of Supper at Emmaus *(1605 - 1606) by Michelangelo Merisi da Caravaggio, Pinacoteca di Brera*

and thematic, moving from the Middle Ages, through the schools of Venice, Lombardy and central northern Italy, from 13-20C. During the visit you will also see the restoration workshops and storage areas.

From the ticket office there is a wonderful view of the reading room in the **Biblioteca Braidense**, founded in 1773 by Maria-Theresa of Austria and designed by Giuseppe Piermarini, the architect of the opera house La Scala. After a number of rooms dedicated to medieval painting, the large **Venetian school** (*rooms 6-14*), of which the Brera collection has the largest number of examples outside of Venice, is represented by masterpieces such as

Pietà★★★ by **Giovanni Bellini**, in which the desert landscape and gunmetal sky echo the tragedy of the subject matter, or the **Dead Christ★★★** by **Mantegna** in which the foreshortening technique accentuates the drama of the painting's realism *(room 6)*. The imposing rooms 8 and 9 house large canvases *(teleri)* by Bellini, Veronese, Tintoretto and Tiziano. The **Jesi** *(room 10)* and **Vitali** collections (room 11) provide an abrupt but intriguing foray into the major international art movements of the first half of the 20th century, featuring iconic works such as Modigliani's *The Fat Child* and *Riot in the Gallery* by Boccioni. The chronological visitor route

BRERA AND CORSO GARIBALDI

0   150   300 m

CORSO COMO
Piazza XXV Aprile
S. Maria Incoronata
Via Volta
Garibaldi
V. Marsala
Castelfidardo
N
Largo la Foppa
Via Moscova
Via D.
Via G.
Via Statuto
Via Solferino
Via San Marco
Via Palermo
Via Montebello
Via Moscova
Via Porta Nuova
Via Porta
Corso
Corso
S. Simpliciano
Via
Via
S. Marco
Via Fatebenefratelli
Via Pontaccio
Via Fiori
Via Chiari
Palazzo Cusani
Via M. Formentini
Via Madonnina
PINACOTECA DI BRERA
Orto Botanico
Via Brera
Via Borgonuovo
Foro Buonaparte
Piazza del Carmine
Palazzo Citterio
V. Fratelli Gabba
Via Ponte Vetero
Via Mercato
Via Moscova

WHERE TO EAT

Cittamani	②
Latteria San Marco	㉑
Pacifico	⑥
Pisacco	㉟
Pizzeria Nazionale	㊽
Princi	㊱
Serendib	㉚

WHERE TO DRINK

Bookshop e Caffetteria degli Atellani	⑨
Bottiglieria Moscatelli	㉚
Bulgari	⑧
Chinese Box	㊵
Farage Cioccolato	㉙
Fioraio Bianchi Caffè	⑪
Le Rosse	㉛
Riva Reno	⑬

SHOPPING

Alfonso Garlando	⑱
Cargo High Tech	㊺
Cavalli & Nastri	⑰
Eataly Milano Smeraldo	㉓
Enoteca Cotti	㉞
Fabriano Boutique	㉟
Profumo	㊲
Traifiori	㊱

NIGHTLIFE

Anteo Palazzo del Cinema	④

resumes in room 12 with the **Lombard school,** represented by the tender **Madonna of the Rose-bush**★★ by Bernardino Luini. In room 22, admire the richness and extraordinary formal elegance of the **works**★ of **Carlo Crivelli**. Room 24 contains three Renaissance masterpieces: the **Montefeltro Altarpiece**★★★ by **Piero della Francesca**, in which an

egg suspended above the characters symbolizes creation and the abstract and geometrical perfection of form sought by the artist, the **Marriage of the Virgin**★★★ by **Raphael**, and the intense **Cristo alla colonna**★★ by **Bramante**. Two rooms on, the magnificent **Supper at Emmaus**★★★ perfectly illustrates the strong contrasts between light and shade, and

the realism, of **Caravaggio**.
After some international paintings
(Rubens, Van Dyck) and Venetian
vedute (Canaletto, Bellotto, Guardi),
there are 19C works: *The Kiss* by **Hayez**,
Fattori's *The Red Cart*, and Giuseppe
da Volpedo's *Fiumana*.
Orto Botanico di Brera – *Entrance on
Via Fratelli Gabba - daily except
Sun 10am-6pm - free*. This compact
botanical garden is a haven of serenity
in the heart of Milan.

SAN MARCO★

Piazza San Marco, 2 - Ⓜ *Lanza -
7am-12pm, 4pm-7pm*.
Until the 1930s, this square was a
waterway intersection (👁 *see inset on
p. 142*); the vast esplanade that flanks
Via San Marco was a large body of
water—the Laghetto di San Marco—
where boats used to dock.
Behind the Gothic façade of pink brick,
restored in the 19C, the neo-classical
interior houses interesting works: the
beautiful frescoes of Paolo Lomazzo
(1571) in the **Foppa chapel** *(1ˢᵗ on right)*,
a paper **crib** from the 18C *(rear of right
nave)* and two Baroque canvases by
Legnanino beside the tranSept The
right wing of the transept houses
Gothic frescoes and the beautiful 14C
sarcophagus of Lanfranco Settala. In
the presbytery and the left wing of
the transept are canvases by the 17C.
Lombard painters **Camillo and Ercole
Procaccini**.
The church, which has wonderful
acoustics and where Mozart and
Giuseppe Verdi both performed, still
hosts concerts today.

BASILICA DI SAN SIMPLICIANO★

Piazza San Simpliciano, 7 - Ⓜ *Lanza -
www.sansimpliciano.it - 7:30am-12pm,
3pm-7pm (4pm-7pm Sun)*.
This is one of the four large basilicas
founded by St Ambrose in the 4C.
Modified in the 10C and 11C, then
reworked in the 19C, it nonetheless
retains the simplicity of the first
Christian buildings. The façade
incorporates a beautiful marble
doorway. The interior, mostly of
brick, is solemn. Note the frescoes
by **Bergognone**, representing *The
Coronation of the Virgin* (1515).

CORSO GARIBALDI

Lined with old buildings with flowers
adorning their courtyards, Corso
Garibaldi is a beautiful, typically
Milanese street filled with bistros,
cafés, bars and trendy stores. Near
the end of the street is **Santa Maria
Incoronata** which can lay claim to
having swallowed up two Gothic
churches. Check out the 15C cloister
and the gorgeous Renaissance-style
hall, with three naves, of the Biblioteca
Umanistica. *Corso Garibaldi 116 - www.
santamariaincoronata.it*.
Turning right into Via Marsala, you
cross Via Solferino before reaching
Via Castelfidardo, which conceals the
last vestiges of a former **sluice-gate**,
surrounded by a garden.
At the end of Corso Garibaldi is **Piazza
XXV Aprile**, which houses the **Porta
Garibaldi** (1826) and offers a fine view
of the skyscrapers of the Porta Nuova
district (👁 *see p. 51*).

Pinacoteca Ambrosiana and old Milan ★★

The area around the famous Pinacoteca Ambrosiana reveals a Milan more in step with the image we traditionally have of Italy: little streets, shops and art galleries, and squares and churches constitute a charming setting. Via Torino, a bustling and more modern street, attracts a younger crowd thanks to its countless clothes shops and department stores.

▶**Getting there:** Ⓜ Duomo (M1 and M3), Cordusio (M1) and Missori (M3). 🚊 2, 3 and 14 on Via Torino.

Map of the area p. 33. Pull-out map DE5-6.

▶**Tip:** Allow half a day.

PINACOTECA AMBROSIANA★★★

Piazza Pio XI, 2 - Ⓜ Cordusio - ✆ 02 806 921 - www.ambrosiana.eu - 10am-6pm - closed Mon - 15 €. Allow 2hrs. This subtly alluring palace is home to one of the most beautiful private collections of paintings in the world. Its construction, completed in 1609, was ordered by cardinal **Federico Borromeo** (👆 *see p. 134)*, who initially wanted to put a public library here, one that later became one of the largest in Europe (500,000 books and 30,000 manuscripts, including the famous *Codice Atlantico* by **Leonardo da Vinci**).

In 26 very well-furnished rooms across two floors, the museum exhibits some of the most important Italian and international artworks of the 15-20C.

1st floor – The first few rooms give an indication of the rich variety of the collection: you'll find **Adoration of the Magi**★ and a *Portrait of a man with armor* by Titian, a delightful **Baby Jesus with lamb**★★ by Bernardino Luini, Botticelli's **Madonna del Padiglione**★★, *Sacra conversazione* by Bergognone and a polyptych by Bartolomeo Vivarini. In room 3, **Enthroned Madonna and child and the saints**★★, by **Bramantino**, is packed with symbols: the giant frog is positioned opposite the character of Arius, swollen and grotesque, a reference to the failure of the Arian heresy that St. Ambrose fought against. Take a moment to admire the rich colors and composition of **The Flight into Egypt** by Jacopo Bassano (1547 - room 4), then head into the room that houses the magnificent **cartoon**★★★ sketched by **Raphael** for *The School of*

WHERE TO EAT

Hostaria Borromei............ 25
Ottimo Massimo............... 39
Peck Italian Bar.................. 18
Trattoria Milanese............ 40

WHERE TO DRINK

Pasticceria Panarello........ 14

SHOPPING

Daniela De Marchi............. 38
Wait and see..................... 21

Athens, the fresco created to decorate the Vatican Rooms in Rome. Room 7 contains the Cardinal's collection of Flemish works: paintings by Paul Brill and Brueghel the Elder's **Allegories of water and fire★★** and the adorable **Mouse, Rose, and Butterfly★**.
The Medusa and Colonne Rooms, decorated between 1929 and 1931, contain a number of intriguing exhibits such as the gloves worn by Napoleon at Waterloo and locks of the hair of Lucrece Borgia and cardinal Borromeo.
2nd floor – This section contains works from the 16-20C, including **portraits★** of **Andrea Appiani** and **Francesco Hayez** and the touching *Chiusi fuori scuola* by Emilio Longoni (1887). Note the expressions on the two girls' faces: the elder child is mortified at being late for school, while the younger one

is delighted to have a whole day off.
Ground floor – Room 24 contains a famous work by **Leonardo da Vinci**: the **Musician★★** which, through its strangely dark background, conveys his desire to establish a relationship between the space and the character in the foreground.
Round off your visit at the library's sublime **Sala Federiciana**, on whose elegant wooden bookshelves you'll find the sketches for the **Codice Atlantico★★★** (1478-1519) by Leonardo da Vinci and, right at the back in splendid isolation, **Basket of fruit★★★** by **Caravaggio**, which elevates the still life to a subject in its own right. Against a monochrome background, coiling leaves and ultra-ripe fruits seem to present the seeds of the notions of aging and death.

CRIPTA DI SAN SEPOLCRO

Piazza San Sepolcro, 1 - ℘ 340 40 85 729 - www.criptasansepolcro milano.it - 5pm-10pm - 10 €.

In the tranquil **Piazza San Sepolcro**, located on top of what was once the **forum** of the Roman city, is the **church** of the same name, founded in the 11C (though its façade was redesigned in the 19C).

Open to the public again after being closed for fifty years, the **crypt** is an evocative place, retaining traces of the forum and the foundations of the church of San Sepolcro.

On the other side of the square, **Palazzo Castani**, built in the 15C. and now home to a police-station, has a beautiful Renaissance-era brick courtyard.

MUSEO MANGINI BONOMI

Via dell'Ambrosiana, 20 - ℘ 02 86 45 14 55 - www.museomanginibonomi - visits by appt. Mon, Wed and Thurs; free after 3pm.

This house-museum boasts an astonishing collection of objects from daily life, collected during the 20C by the passionate and tasteful collector **Emilio Carlo Mangini** and his son Giuseppe. In a splendid residence from the 15C you'll find objects associated with private life, work and leisure (games, musical instruments, walking sticks, keys, purses, lamps, etc.). The last two floors contain original items from the apartment of Emilio Mangini.

PIAZZA BORROMEO

On Borromeo square, across from the Santa Maria Podone church, **Palazzo Borromeo** built in the 15C by the banker Vitaliano Borromeo, has two courts with arcades, restored to their exact previous condition after the bombing raids of 1943. All that remains of the magnificent interior decoration are the famous **frescoes★★ in the games room** (15C): scenes depicting tarot, ball games, and public figures, on a red, pink and ochre background, bear witness to the life of the era in an exceptional manner. *Now containing an office, the room can be seen on weekdays through a window, between 8am and 6:30pm; ask an employee and they will let you take a look.*

The charming nearby streets of **San Maurilio** and **Santa Marta** are lined with colorful old apartment buildings housing galleries, antique shops and stores selling all manner of items. Note the cast iron balconies, a typically Milanese feature.

SAN GIORGIO AL PALAZZO

Piazza San Giorgio - Ⓜ Missori - 7:30am-12pm, 3:30pm-6:30pm, Sun 9:30am-12pm, 4pm-7pm.

A short walk from bustling **Via Torino**, in a little square, is the neo-classical façade of this church, dominated by a slim steeple and an elegant cupola. There is a sublime work by Bernardino Luini inside with beautiful colors, the **Christ Carrying the Cross★** (1516).

SANT'ALESSANDRO★

*Piazza Sant'Alessandro - ⓜ Missori -
☎ 02 72 21 71 - 8:30am-11:30am,
2:30pm-6:30pm, Sun 10:30am-12pm,
6pm-7pm.*

The grandiose Baroque façade of this
church, like a set design at a theater,
with its two towers and its angels,
stands opposite the monumental gates
of the 18C. **Palazzo Trivulzio**.
The church, erected in the early 17C,
is a very fine example of Milanese
Baroque. It is dominated by a
beautifully proportioned dome. The
interior★, with its abundance of
marble, frescoes and gildings, houses
numerous works by 18C painters from
Lombardy. The pulpit and main altar
are particularly impressive. In the far
bottom-right corner, the **Cappella
della Natività** has a remarkable roof
by **Camillo Procaccini** and frescoes by
Moncalvo.

❯ *Head back to Via Torino, via Via
Lupetta.*

The **Rotonda di San Sebastiano** was
built by Pellegrino Tibaldi in 1576 as an
ex-voto, as a sign of gratitude for the
fact that the plague had ended.

SANTA MARIA PRESSO
SAN SATIRO★

*Via Speronari,3 - ⓜ Duomo -
9:30am-5:30pm, Sun 2pm-5:30pm.*
The church is dedicated to Satiro, the
brother of St. Ambrose. The church's
origins date back to the 9C. The
plain façade from 1871, at the back

of a small recess, hides a major work
from the Italian Renaissance, by the
architect **Bramante**. The interior, with
its three naves, offers an unsettling
and unusual perspective on the **false
choir★★**, scarcely 1m deep but made
to seem deeper using the trompe-l'œil
technique. The **baptistry★** *(enter from
the right-hand nave)* and the **cupola★**
are also remarkable.
The basilica incorporates the **Saccello
di San Satiro** *(visible from the left
transept)*, a small Byantine-style
sanctuary in the shape of a Greek
cross, adorned with a polychrome
terracotta *Descente de Croix* (15C) and
fragments of frescoes (9-12C).
From Via Falcone, which runs along
the apse of the church, you can admire
the Lombard Roman **campanile**, built
out of brick in the 9C, and the exterior
of the Pietà chapel, which houses the
Saccello di San Satiro.

VIA SPADARI

Lined with splendid Liberty-style
balconies, this street is the 'Via del
Gusto' ('taste street'). It contains great
names from Italian gastronomy, like
Peck, the 'Fauchon of Milan' (❖ *see
'Where to eat' p. 93)* and Pescheria
Spadari, one of the most famous (and
luxurious) fishmonger's in Milan.

Ca' Granda and the former canals★

Visible at various points on Via Francesco Sforza and Via Visconti di Modrone is one of the canals that surrounded the city center up until 1930. This district has a remarkable heritage. On weekdays it's a hive of activity, as the university, the Ospedale Maggiore and the palace of justice are here, but this all changes when the work week is done. On weekends you can enjoy peace and quiet in the green spaces, like the Giardino della Guastalla, and in the secret alleyways that wind their way between the wide, solemn avenues.

▶**Getting there:** Ⓜ Missori (M3); San Babila (M1), bus 94 on Via Francesco Sforza and Via Visconti di Modrone. Don't forget that the city center is classed as Area C, so you have to pay 5 €/day to travel around it.

Map of the area p. 38. Pull-out map EG4-6.

▶**Tip:** Allow half a day. On Via San Barnaba, you'll find a very handy parking garage (2 €/hr, minimum 2h. and discount on the Area C charge: 3 € rather than 5 €). In this part of town there is construction taking place on metro line 4, so it's best to walk there from the Piazza Duomo (10min).

SAN GIOVANNI IN CONCA

Piazza Missori - Ⓜ Missori - 9:30am-5pm - free entry.
This is a pretty extraordinary place: in the middle of **Piazza Missori**, you'll find a stairway leading down to the former Roman crypt of a basilica founded in the 11C. The church, redesigned several times, was demolished in the 19C and 20C. to enable Via Mazzini and the Piazza Missori to be opened. The façade was reused for the Waldensian temple in Via Francesco Sforza.

TORRE VELASCA★★

Piazza Velasca, 5 - Ⓜ Missori.
This pink tower, which dominates the area with its height of 106 m, is one of the most iconic skyscrapers in Milan. Built with reinforced concrete in 1956 by the architects Belgioioso, Peresutti and Rogers, it is known for nine overhanging floors at the top, giving it the silhouette of a medieval tower.

SAN NAZARO★

Piazza San Nazaro in Brolo, 5 - Ⓜ Missori - 8am-12pm, 3pm-6pm.
This former Roman basilica from the 12C was completed in the 16C. Lovely sober interior in the Lombard Roman

© Pierre Jacques/hemis.fr

Università degli Studi di Milano - Statale

style, and numerous traces of frescoes. The **Cappella di Santa Caterina** (*enter via the left transept*) contains some remarkable **frescoes** by Bernardino Larino (1546).

Turn left and walk around the building to admire the apse and the arcade-porticoes of the university.

CA' GRANDA - UNIVERSITÀ★★

Via Festa del Perdono, 5 - Ⓜ Missori.
What is now the university was originally a hospital, founded by Francesco and Bianca Sforza in 1456 to a design by **Filarete**. The building was redesigned several times. t has a long brick façade that runs all the way along Via Festa del Perdono, enlivened by twin-windows, Renaissance arcades and sculpted busts inside medallions. The **main courtyard** (created by Richini) is superb, with its floors of galleries with arcades, redesigned in the 17C. On the right, enter the Renaissance courtyards, laid out around two cross-shaped corridors.

SANT'ANTONIO ABATE

Via Sant'Antonio Abate, 5 - 10am-6pm (2pm in winter).
The unassuming façade of this church conceals a superb **interior**★, a fine example of Milan's first Baroque period. Head into the pretty cloister

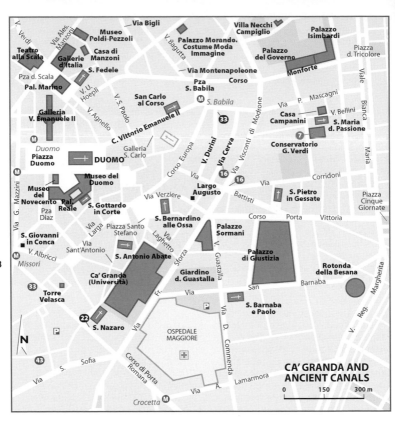

CA' GRANDA AND
ANCIENT CANALS

0   150   300 m

38

WHERE TO EAT	WHERE TO DRINK	SHOPPING
Al Mercato..................................**43**	Pasticceria Giovanni Galli......................**33**	Brian&Barry..................................**33**
Bottiglieria da Pino..................................**16**	Taveggia......................................**16**	Danese......................................**22**
		NIGHTLIFE
		Conservatorio..............................**7**

(to the left of the church) to admire the terracotta Renaissance arcades.
At no. 12 in the same street, Palazzo Greppi dates from the late 18C; check out its beautiful main courtyard.

PIAZZA SANTO STEFANO

On this quiet square are the **Santo Stefano**, dating from the 16th c., and the church **San Bernardino alle Ossa**. Octagonal in shape, it has an unusual **chapel★** *(7:30am-12pm, 1pm-6pm)* whose walls are covered with human bones and Baroque frescoes.
Via Laghetto is one of the oldest streets in the historic center and offers an intriguing view of the cathedral and its spire.

GIARDINO DELLA GUASTALLA

Via Francesco Sforza and Via San Barnaba - Ⓜ *Missori.*
This little garden, designed in the 16C is a verdant oasis. Its pool, lined with balustrades, statues and decorative edifices, offers lovely views of the surrounding monuments. Note the church **Santi Barnaba e Paolo** (with its Renaissance façade), the **synagogue** with its fine mosaic façade (1892) and the tall tower of **Palazzo di Giustizia**, built from 1932 to 1940 by Marcello Piacentini and Ernesto Rapisardi, in a very pompous rationalist style.

ROTONDA DELLA BESANA

Via Enrico Besana, 12 - ℘ *02 43 98 04 02 - www.muba.it.*
This vast ensemble dating from the 18C, once the cemetery of the nearby hospital, now houses **MUBA (Museo dei Bambini)**, a space dedicated to children that also hosts temporary exhibitions.

LARGO AUGUSTO

Palazzo Sormani (17C), whose **rear façade★**, overlooking the park, is remarkable *(visible from Via Francesco Sforza)* houses one of the largest libraries in the city.
A little farther on, on the left, is the Largo Augusto, which was once a herb market (the **Verziere**). The column (1580) was erected to celebrate the end of the plague in 1577.
On Corso di Porta Vittoria is the church **San Pietro in Gessate** (15C); inside is the Grifi chapel, decorated with **frescoes★** about the life of St. Ambrose, by Bernardino Butinone and Bernardino Zenale. *7am-12pm, 3pm-6pm.*

SANTA MARIA DELLA PASSIONE★★

Via del Conservatorio - Ⓜ *San Babila - 8am-12pm, 3:30pm-6pm, Sun 9:30am-12:30pm, 3:30pm-6:30pm.*
Built between the late 15C and the 18C, this huge church with its Baroque façade has a large, bright interior, adorned with paintings from different eras but with the same subject: the passion of the Christ. Note the tall cupola attributed to Lombardo (1530). In the left transept is a very fine painting by Gaudenzio Ferrari representing *The Last Supper*. The chapter house is decorated with

Street with the Conservatorio Giuseppe Verdi

40

frescoes by Bergognone, dating from the late 15C.
Beside it, the former monastery of Santa Maria della Passione houses the prestigious **Conservatorio Giuseppe Verdi**.
To the left of the church, at no. 11, Via Bellini, admire the superb **Casa Campanini★**, in the Liberty style.

CORSO MONFORTE

There are some splendid palaces on this street. At no. 32, there's a fine interpretation of Liberty by Campanini; at no. 35, **Palazzo Isimbardi** with a

superb 16C arcade-lined patio; at no. 31, **Palazzo del Governo** featuring a beautiful Neo-Classical courtyard adorned with caryatids.
Round off your visit by walking along **Via Durini**, **Via Cerva** and the old streets around them, where enticing shops alternate with majestic palaces.

FONDAZIONE PRADA★

Pull-out map G8
Largo Isarco, 2 - Ⓜ Lodi or Tram *24 leaving from Corso di Porta Romana (stop Via Ripamonti/Via Lorenzini) - ℘ 02 56 66 26 12 - www.fondazioneprada.org - 10am-9pm - 10 €.*
The Dutch architect **Rem Koolhaas** turned a former distillery built in the 1910s into a multi-purpose site. The new site is broken down into rooms dedicated to the Fondazione's permanent collection of contemporary art, constructions designed to house temporary exhibitions, a movie theater, a library and public spaces; note the very pretty café **Bar Luce**, designed by the director Wes Anderson who recreates the atmosphere of the cafés of old Milan. Opened in May 2015, the Fondazione quickly became a focal point in the city's cultural life.

© BrasilNut1/iStockphoto.com

Porta Ticinese, Navigli and Solari district★★

This district, very popular with young people, is also one of the oldest districts in the city, as you can tell from the magnificent Roman columns of the San Lorenzo basilica. Always animated, it is a place where culture, shopping and leisure can be combined, for the benefit of locals and tourists alike.

▶**Getting there:** Ⓜ Sant'Agostino and Porta Genova (M2); [Tram] 2 (Via Cesare Correnti and Corso Genova), 3 (Via Torino and Corso di Porta Ticinese) and 14 (Via Cesare Correnti, Corso Genova, Via Solari).

Map of the area p. 44. Pull-out map AE6-7.

▶**Tip:** allow half a day. Set aside time for a boat trip to discover the Navigli.

41

BASILICA DI SAN LORENZO MAGGIORE★★

Corso di Porta Ticinese, 35 - ℘ 02 89 40 41 29 - www.sanlorenzomaggiore. com - 8am-6:30pm, Sun 9am-7pm - Cappella di Sant'Aquilino 2 €.

The **Colonne di San Lorenzo★**, the last vestiges of a gate with sixteen columns and a rare trace of the Roman city of Mediolanum, marks the entrance to one of the city's major basilicas. San Lorenzo was founded back in the 4C when Milan was the capital of the Roman Empire: it was probably the Palatine basilica, part of the lost imperial palace. Fires in the 11C and 12C. altered its structure, and the grandiose cupola had to be rebuilt after it collapsed in 1573. The façade is a monumental creation dating from 1894.

The majestic interior, in the Roman-Byzantine style, is surrounded by matronea (places reserved for women in the churches), topped with a vast cupola and with a wide circumference. To the right of the choir, an atrium and a Roman door from the 1C. provide access to the **Cappella di Sant'Aquilino★★**, built in the 5C. as an imperial mausoleum (there is still a magnificent sarcophagus here, of unknown origins). The chapel houses frescoes from the 12C and 14C and splendid **Paleochristian mosaics★** dating from the 5C, one of which represents Christ and the apostles. Behind the altar with the urn containing the remains of St. Aquiline, a staircase leads to the foundations of the building.

From **Piazza della Vetra** you can admire the remarkable apse and the beautiful proportions of the basilica. If you walk into its extension, beyond Via Molino delle Armi, you can stroll through **Parco delle Basiliche** to reach Sant'Eustorgio.

Make a little detour to see a hidden gem: **Parco dell'Anfiteatro**, tucked away between Via De Amicis and Via Arena, holds the ruins of a Roman amphitheater from the 1C. *Via De Amicis, 17 - 9am-6pm (4:30pm in winter) - closed Sat pm and Sun - free.*

CORSO DI PORTA TICINESE

This wide thoroughfare, which takes you to the gate of the same name and to the Navigli, has a large number of small designers and youngish fashion boutiques. There are also bars and restaurants that fit the same bill.

Museo Diocesano – *Corso di Porta Ticinese, 95 - Ⓜ Porta Genova - ℰ 02 89 42 00 19 - http:// chiostrisanteustorgio.it - 10am-6pm - closed Mon - 8 € including admission to Cappella Portinari.* This museum, with its very contemporary design, exhibits some remarkable examples of 16-19C. Lombard painting.

BASILICA DI SANT'EUSTORGIO★

Piazza Sant'Eustorgio, 1 - ℰ 02 58 10 15 83 - 7:30am-12pm, 3:30pm-6:30pm. The basilica, which dates back to the 5-6C, as we know from the ruins of the apse and the Roman-era Christian **necropolis** *(the ticket for the Cappella Portinari entitles you to see it, see below),* is a blend of different eras today. The **interior** contains beautiful chapels created for the city's

important families, like the **Cappella Viscontea** *(4th from bottom on the right)* with its pretty 13C The right-hand transept houses the **Cappella dei Magi★** with the sarcophagus that supposedly houses the relics of the Magi. According da *The Golden Legend* by Jacques de Voragine, St. Helena, the Emperor Constantine's mother, found these relics in around 330 and took them to Constantinople, from whence they were taken to Milan by the bishop Eustorgius. After Milan was defeated and demolished in 1162 by Barbarossa, the remains of the Magi were supposedly transported to Cologne in 1164. Some of the relics were taken to Milan in 1904 and now rest, it is said, in this sarcophagus. Watching over the central nave is a monumental wooden **crucifix** from the 13C. The remarkable **polyptych of the Passion★**, made for Galeazzo Visconti in the 14C, with a crucifix attributed to Jacopino da Tradate at its center, adorns the main altar.

Behind the manse is a sort of crypt containing the ruins of Paleochristian walls.

Cappella Portinari★★ – *Access from the left-hand nave or from Piazza Sant'Eustorgio, 3 - ℰ 02 89 40 26 7 - 8 € ticket includes admission to the Museo Diocesano.* The chapel is a jewel of the Lombard Renaissance embellished with superb **frescoes** from the 15C by **Vincenzo Foppa**, depicting the life of St. Peter of Verona, Dominican monk and Inquisitor, who died from a sickle-blow to the head in an ambush in 1252. With its Bramantesque central plan, it boasts perfect proportions. At its center is

the magnificent **arch of St. Peter the martyr★★**, in marble, sculpted by Giovanni di Balduccio in the 14C one of the greatest works of Gothic Italian sculpture. The painted decoration on the cupola represents the radiation of divine light.

DARSENA AND NAVIGLI★

Ⓜ *Porta Genova - excursions by boat leaving from Alzaia Naviglio Grande, 4 - ℘ 02 90 94 242 - http://*

www.naviglilombardi.it/navigare/ in-barca - 55mins.

On **Piazza XXIV Maggio** are the **Porta Ticinese**, from medieval times, and the buildings of the former customs house. Stretching out from there is the **darse**, Milan's former port, which, after renovation work, became the city's river port once again in 2015, with a pretty little market and spacious embankments that are popular in the warmer months.

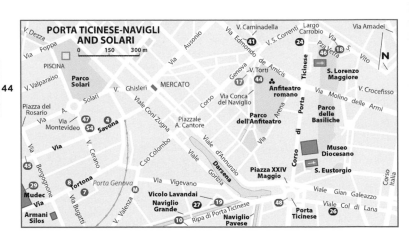

44

WHERE TO EAT			
Al Fresco	㊺	Panino Lab alla Ferramenta	㊼
Cantina della Vetra	㊻	Rebelot	⑩
Drogheria Milanese	㊹		
Enrico Bartolini al Mudec	㉙	**WHERE TO DRINK**	
Esco Bistrò Mediterraneo	⑧	La Hora Feliz	⑱
Gino Sorbillo - Olio a Crudo	㊴	El Brellin Caffè	⑲
Kiosko II	㊽	Liquidambar	⑦
Langosteria 10	④		

SHOPPING	
Frip	㉔
Mercatone dell'Antiquariato	㉗
Wag	㊶
Wok Store	㉖

NIGHTLIFE	
Le Biciclette	⑰

Setting off from here almost at a right-angle are **Naviglio Grande** (50 km long) and **Naviglio Pavese** (33 km), the last two remaining canals of the system built in the 16C, by Leonardo da Vinci and others, to connect Milan to the Po and the great lakes.
If you follow the **Alzaia Naviglio Grande** beside the first and most evocative canal, you discover an extraordinary aspect of the city: houses with colored façades, little bridges straddling the canal and the charming **Vicolo dei Lavandai**, with the former laundrette used until the start of the 1960s. Approximately 800 m farther on, the church of **San Cristoforo** is a ravishing ensemble composed of two brick churches, from the 12-15C This is one of the most happening places in Milan, particularly in the evening. There is an antiques market here on the last Sunday of the month *(www.navigliogrande.mi.it)*.
Alzaia Naviglio Pavese, beside the other canal, is less distinctive but quieter.

SOLARI DISTRICT

Ⓜ *Porta Genova*. West of the Navigli, the area around **Parco Solari** is a heartland for design and fashion; the galleries and boutiques are concentrated around **Via Tortona** and **Via Savona**. Industrial wastelands converted into loft-spaces and exhibition spaces rub shoulders with **case di ringhiera**, the popular old apartment buildings whose apartments open onto external passageways. **Superstudio Più** (*Via Tortona, 27*), 13,000 m² of rooms, warehouses, open-air spaces and photographic studios, is the home of major events in fashion and design.
Via Bergognone is the fiefdom of **Giorgio Armani**: the label's head office is at no. 59 along with the **Teatro Armani** designed by the Japanese Tadao Ando, while at no. 40 is **Armani Silos**, an exhibition space for the couturier's creations.
☏ 02 91 63 00 10 - www.armanisilos. com - Wed-Sun 11am-7pm - 12 €.
Fans of the architecture of the 1930s to 1960s should visit Via Solari, Via Foppa, Via Dezza (where the famous architect Gio Ponti lived) and Piazza del Rosario.

MUDEC
(MUSEO DELLE CULTURE)★

45

Via Tortona, 56 - Ⓜ Porta Genova - ☏ 02 54 917 - www.muDecit - 9:30am-7:30pm (Thurs and Sat 10:30pm) - closed Mon and Tue - 5 €, 12 € for temporary exhibitions.
Located in a building once used by the **Ansaldo factories** (1910-1930), this remarkable complex, designed by **David Chipperfield**, has an ultra-contemporary setting, yet preserves its original structures. It offers temporary exhibitions, a permanent section on ethnographic art, a bistro, design store, gourmet restaurant and, thankfully, a parking lot!

Sant'Ambrogio and Corso Magenta★★

While a cacophany of clattering orange trams accompanies you all the way along Corso Magenta to the bustling Corso Vercelli (one of the locals' favorite shopping streets on a Saturday afternoon), St. Ambrose basilica stands in a far quieter part of town. In this enticing haven of peace, a quasi-city within the city, even the students of the nearby Cattolica university seem reluctant to disturb the serenity of the centuries-old stones.

▶**Getting there:** Ⓜ Conciliazione (M1); Cadorna (M1 and M2) and Sant'Ambrogio (M2). 🚋 16 (Corso Magenta).
Map of the area p. 48. Pull-out map AC4-5.
▶**Tip:** allow half a day.

MUSEO NAZIONALE DELLA SCIENZA E DELLA TECNOLOGIA LEONARDO DA VINCI★★

Via San Vittore, 21 - Ⓜ Sant'Ambrogio - 🕿 02 48 55 51 - www.museoscienza.org - 9:30am-5pm (6:30pm on w/ends) - closed Mon - 10 € + sottomarino Toti 8 € (booking via the website recommended).
Located inside the former monastery San Vittore, it houses the **Leonardo da Vinci gallery★** where sketches for some of the inventions he dreamed up are displayed. The other sections of the museum are dedicated to acoustics, chemistry, telecommunications, astronomy and space exploration. The pavilions focusing on maritime transport and railroads are very impressive. Adults and kids alike will enjoy looking around the submarine known as **Toti**, the first one to be built in Italy after the Second World War. Built in the late 16th c., the church **San Vittore al Corpo**, adjoining the museum, has a remarkably rich **interior★** from the 17C Inside are the ruins of an imperial mausoleum from the 4-5C. *7:30am-12pm, 3:30pm-6:30pm - closed Sun afternoon.*

▶ *Walk down Via San Vittore.*

On the corner of Via Carducci, note the eclectic **Castello Cova**, built in 1910 by the architect Adolfo Coppedè (1871-1951).

BASILICA DI SANT'AMBROGIO★★★

Piazza Sant'Ambrogio, 15 - Ⓜ Sant'Ambrogio - 🕿 02 86 45 08 95 - www.basilica santambrogio.it - 10am-12pm, 2:30pm-6pm, Sun 3pm-5pm.

© C. Labonne/Michelin

Mosaics, Basilica di Sant'Ambrogio

The basilica, one of Roman art's great European masterpieces, was founded in the late 4C by Bishop Ambrose (♻ *see info box p. 136*) so that the bodies of the martyrs Gervasius and Protasius could be placed inside (they're kept in a silver shrine in the crypt) and acquired its definitive form in the 11C and 12C. The façade and towers form an original tableau. The way in is via the **atrium**★, whose arcades rest on beautiful capitals. Among the remarkable works here is the eye-catching 12C. **Byzantine altar**★ atop a 4C sarcophagus. The magnificent **altar cloth**★★, with its gold and silver discs, is a masterpiece of the Carolingian period (9C). The huge mosaic in the apse (12C) was re-assembled after the Second World War. Not to be missed is the **treasury**, in the far-right corner, where you'll see the ancient **Cappella di San Vittore in Ciel d'Oro**. Built in the 5C to house the remains of St. Victor the martyr, it is adorned with remarkable **mosaics**★. At the back of the left-hand nave, you can pass through a portico attributed to Bramante.

SAN MAURIZIO★★

Corso Magenta, 13 - ⓜ *Cadorna -* ☎ *02 88 44 52 08 - 9:30am-5:30pm, Sun*
Built in the 16C, the church in the Benedictine monastery has a sober façade. Its interior, by contrast, is incredible and features splendid

48

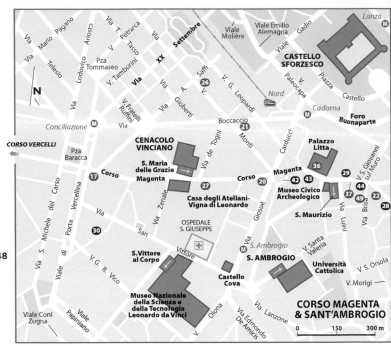

frescoes★★ by **Bernardino Luini**: paintings of saints and scenes from the Passion of Christ provide wonderfully vivid decoration from floor to ceiling. Via a passage located in the far-left corner, you can access the **Coro delle Monache**, where classical music concerts are held.

MUSEO ARCHEOLOGICO★

Corso Magenta, 15 - Ⓜ Cadorna - ℘ 02 88 46 57 20 - 9am-5:30pm - closed Mon - 5 € or Tourist MuseumCard (👍 see p. 128).

The museum, housed in what is left of the former Benedictine monastery, has collections of Greek, Etruscan, Roman and barbarian art, which amount to a formidable source of information about ancient life. The Roman section contains the site's two masterpieces: the **Coppa Trivulzio★** (4C AD), a cup fashioned out of a single piece of glass, and the **Patera di Parabiago★** (4C AD), a huge silver dish adorned with images depicting the goddess Cybele. In the garden, the ruins of the Roman city walls remind us that Milan was the capital of the Western Roman Empire at the end of the 3th c. (👍 see p. 136). Across from here, the **Palazzo Litta** (17-18C.) has a beautiful rococo façade complete with atlantes. It contains a theater and some beautifully decorated rooms.

Near the museum, on Via Brisa, are the ruins of the **imperial palace** dating from the 3-4C.

SANTA MARIA DELLE GRAZIE★★

Piazza Santa Maria delle Grazie - Ⓜ Conciliazione - ℘ 02 467 61 11 - http://legraziemilano.it - 7am-12pm, 3:30pm-7pm.

The Renaissance church, built by the Dominicans from 1465 to 1490 in a pretty little square, was designed by **Bramante**, it is one of the masterpieces of the Milanese Renaissance. In 1943, the church was severely damaged by a bomb and had to undergo many years of restoration; the bomb spared its two great treasures, however - Leonardo da Vinci's *The Last Supper* and Bramante's marvelous **tribune★★**. The interior is adorned with **decorations** painted in the late 15C. The side chapels are sumptuously decorated too: note the frescoes by Gaudenzio Ferrari *(4th chapel on the right)* and the manificent decoration of the **sixteen-sided cupola★**. To the left of the apse, the chapel of the Madonna delle Grazie houses the highly venerated image for which the church is named.

On the left side of the transept is the charming **cloister★** by Bramante, particularly popular in early spring, when the magnolias are in bloom.

CENACOLO VINCIANO★★★

Piazza Santa Maria delle Grazie, 2 - Ⓜ Conciliazione - ℘ 02 92 80 03 60 - www.vivaticket.it - 8:15am-6:45pm - closed Mon - Booking mandatory (well in advance) - 6.50 € + 1.50 € booking fee. - 15-min. visit per group.

The convent's former refectory *(cenacolo)* contains one of the most famous paintings in the world, **The**

49

Last Supper by **Leonardo da Vinci**, painted between 1485 and 1497, at the request of Ludovico Il Moro. A clever and dramatic composition (with trompe-l'oeil making it appear longer than it is), it portrays the very first Eucharist. The technique used (*a tempera* painting, perhaps mixed with oil, and chose to paint on the coldest wall in the room), the fact that a bomb fell on the refectory in 1943, exposing the work to dust and bad weather, and pollution have necessitated various kinds of restoration work. The most recent campaign lasted 21 years and was completed in 1999. The perspective and the movement of the apostles around Jesus are captivating. Note, too, the beautiful fresco of the **Crucifixion★** by **Montorfano** (1495).

VIGNA DI LEONARDO AND CASA DEGLI ATELLANI

Corso Magenta, 65 - ☎ 02 48 16 150 - www.vignadileonardo.com - 9am-6pm - 10 € with audio-guide - booking advisable, esp. w/end.
The **house of the Atellani** dates from the late 15C, when Ludovico il Moro gave this family, who showed him great loyalty, two houses in a district full of vegetable patches and gardens reserved for courtesans. The property eventually ended up in the hands of the entrepreneur Ettore Conti (1871-1972), who entrusted the task of renovating it to his son-in-law **Piero Portaluppi**, one of the greatest Italian architects of the 20C. The result is a harmonious **residence★** that still has

Renaissance-era frescoes and decor, making it rather unique in Milan. A **vineyard** of approx. 1 ha, given to Leonardo da Vinci in 1498 by Ludovico il Moro and on which da Vinci grew malvoisie, used to be where the current **garden** is; it was replanted with great philological rigor by the Portaluppi foundation in 2015, creating a charmingly rustic spot.

VIA XX SETTEMBRE

Take Via Fratelli Ruffini to reach a pretty district where the beautiful streets are organized around **Via XX Settembre** and the harmonious **Piazza Tommaseo**. There are apartment buildings and residences from the late 19 and early 20C. (Via Saffi, Via Tamburini, Via Rovani). From here, it's a short walk to the very commercial **Corso Vercelli**.

CITYLIFE

Off pull-out map, beyond A3.
Farther along Via Gabriele Rossetti (20 mins from Santa Maria delle Grazie). This new residential area at the old Fiera di Milano site is centered around iconic skyscrapers: the **Torre Allianz** (Arata Isozaki) dubbed *The Straight One*, **Torre Generali** (Zaha Hadid), *The Twisted One*, and Torre Libeskind (Daniel Libeskind, coming in 2020), *The Curved One*. Beyond this are a pretty **park** and a shopping mall.

Porta Nuova and northern districts★

Welcome to the Milan of the future, a mini-Manhattan that has already won the hearts of the Milanese (and of the Qatari emirs who bought it for what was said to be an enormous sum). While the city's four other districts focus above all on its past, here we find ourselves among brand new green spaces and state-of-the-art skyscrapers that have already garnered international awards.

▶**Getting there:** Ⓜ Garibaldi (M2 and M5), Isola (M5), Monumentale (M5), Cenisio (M5) and Centrale (M1 and M3).
Pull-out map EG 1-2.
▶**Tip:** Allow half a day. On Sundays, don't miss the chance to go up to the terrace of the Palazzo Lombardia, with its panoramic views.

CORSO COMO

Beyond **Piazza XXV Aprile** is **Corso Como**, a pedestrianized road that has become one of the centers of Milanese *movida*, with multiple clubs and lounge bars as well as the famous **Corso Como 10**, the concept store from gallery owner Carla Sozzani, dedicated to art, design and fashion (♿ *see p. 112*). A few steps from Piazza 25 Aprile are the brand new headquarters of the **Fondazione Feltrinelli**, which also house a store, a library and an exhibition space. *Viale Pasubio, 5 - 9am-1pm, 1:30pm-6pm.*

PIAZZA GAE AULENTI★ AND THE PORTA NUOVA DISTRICT

E1-2 Designed by twenty international architects, the **Porta Nuova** project, launched in the 2000s, transformed the vast zone stretching between Garibaldi station, Piazza della Repubblica and the Stazione Centrale. It contains skyscrapers, green spaces, art centers, offices and businesses. With its excellent location and boasting ample infrastructure, pedestrianized zones and cycle-paths, the area began attracting locals, tourists and investors alike. Previously more of a working-class area, it quickly became 'gentrified', with chic boutiques, hipster cafés and Michelin-starred restaurants springing up.
The **Isola district**, north of Garibaldi station, has a younger and more dynamic vibe, with nightclubs, studios and bistros.
The beating heart of Porta Nuova is **Piazza Gae Aulenti★**, an elevated circular agora with a very happening vibe, beside which Unicredit built its head office in 2012 in the **Torre Unicredit**, a curved skyscraper

designed by the architect **Cesare Pelli** and ranking as Italy's tallest (231m).

The skyscrapers

Porta Nuova also has a residential section, whose flagship building is the **Bosco Verticale★** ("vertical wood"), designed by Studio Boeri, which won the International Highrise Award in 2014. Its residential towers, 76 and 110m tall respectively, have almost a thousand plants built into their façades, the equivalent of one hectare of woodland.

The **Torre Diamante** (Kohn Pederson Fox Studio, 2012) looks out from its multi-sided façade over the Viale della Liberazione and the Piazza della Repubblica.

Not far away is the imposing complex of the **Palazzo Lombardia** (Pei Cobb Freed & Partners, New York, 2011), new HQ of the Lombardy Region. On Sundays, there's free entry to the panoramic terrace on the 39th floor, with its **unbeatable view★★** of the city. *Piazza Città di Lombardia - Sun 10am-6pm - free.*

Slightly farther east, towards the station, you can see the elegant silhouette of the **Grattacielo Pirelli★** (127m tall). A precursor—along with the **Torre Breda** in Piazza della Repubblica (1954)—of the skyscrapers recently built here, the 'Pirellone' (1956-1960) is the masterpiece of the great Milanese architect **Gio Ponti** (1891-1979).

STAZIONE CENTRALE★

G1 *Piazza Duca d'Aosta -* Ⓜ *Centrale.*
Made in 1912-1931 by the architect Ulisse Stacchini, in an eclectic style, this building blends the Liberty style with Fascist architecture.
On the station's right flank is **Memoriale della Shoah**, an important reminder that on platform 21, below the ground, Jews and opponents of the Fascist regime were loaded into railway cars to be sent to the camps of Auschwitz-Birkenau and Bergen Belsen. *Largo Safra, 1 - ℘ 02 28 20 975 - www.memorialeshoah.it.*

CIMITERO MONUMENTALE★

CD1 *Piazzale Cimitero Monumentale 1 -* Ⓜ *Monumentale - ℘ 02 88 46 56 00 - 8am-6pm - closed Mon.*
This 19C cemetery, a Neo-Gothic work by Carlo Maciachini, is well worth going to see due to the magnificence of its tombstones, some of which are veritable palaces, created by sculptors like Mosè Bianchi, Medardo Rosso, Francesco Messina and Giacomo Manzù. Among those buried here are the writer Alessandro Manzoni, the painter Francesco Hayez and the musician Arturo Toscanini.

CHINESE QUARTER

CD2 With its fashion boutiques and Asian grocery stores, Milan's Chinatown is at its liveliest around **Via Paolo Sarpi**, where you will also find hip bistros and bars.

Torre Unicredit designed by Cesare Pelli. Picture Ca' so Andreis

The abbeys and Monza★

A short distance from the frenzy of the city center are some real havens of peace. Abbeys, chapter houses and gardens attest to the intense activity of the monastic orders on the territory, in the Middle Ages and the Renaissance. A few kilometers from Milan, a wonderful adventure awaits you in the city of Monza.

▶ **Getting there:** Monza is easy to get to by train (15-20min), leaving from the Stazione Garibaldi. If coming by car take Viale Zara and Viale Fulvio Testi, then the SP 58. You will need a car if you wish to visit the abbeys.

Map of Lombardy and the Lakes region (inside the cover) B2.

▶ **Tip:** allow half a day for the abbeys and half a day for Monza.

CERTOSA DI GAREGNANO★

B2 Via Garegnano, 28, 5 km north-west of the center (take Viale Certosa) - ℘ 02 38 00 6301 - 9:30am-12pm (except Sun), 3:30pm-5:15pm.
A former chapter house from the 15th-16th c., it has a tranquil courtyard that pre-dates the superb Renaissance façade. Inside are some lovely Baroque frescoes by the Lombard painter **Daniele Crespi** (17C).

ABBAZIA DI CHIARAVALLE★★

B2 Via Sant'Arialdo, 102, 7 km south-east of the center; exit via the Porta Romana - ℘ 0523 94 01 32 - www.chiaravalledellacolomba.it - 8:30am-12pm, 2:30pm-6:30pm.
Built in 1135 by St. Bernard de Clairvaux (hence its name), this **abbey** marks the arrival of Gothic architecture in Italy. Adorned with white stones in the Cistercian style, it is dominated by an elegant polygonal **bell-tower**★★ ; the porch was added in the 17C.

The interior is topped with a cupola adorned with 14C. In the right-hand crosspiece, a fresco depicts the Tree of Benedictine saints. The cloister is full of charm.

ABBAZIA DI VIBOLDONE★

B2 Via dell'Abbazia, 7 - San Giuliano Milanese, 13 km south-east of the center; take Via Emilia, then turn right (signposted) - ℘ 02 98 41 203 - www.viboldone.it - 5:25am-12:30pm, 2:30pm-6:30pm.
This oasis of calm, where a Benedictine community once lived, was founded in 1176. On its façade, which has elements of the Lombard and Gothic styles, the *Madonna and Child* on the door is the work of *maestri campionesi*. Inside are some remarkable **frescoes**★★ remarquables (in the right-hand nave, *Madonna and Child with saints* attributed to Michelino da Besozzo, 1395). The *Last Judgment* (1350) is a masterpiece by Giusto de' Menabuoi, a pupil of Giotto, also active in Padua.

Royal Monza

Monza, close to Milan, with a population of 122,900, has a surprisingly rich heritage, but a little background history explains everything. In 590, Queen Theodelinda, widow of the king of the Lombards, Authari, married Agilulf and made Monza the summer residence of the Lombard court (which ruled from Milan); she had the duomo of Monza built, and it houses the precious iron crown. The symbol of Italian royalty, it was used, for this reason, by Charlemagne and all the Germanic emperors, as well as by Napoleon at the time of his self-coronation as King of Italy in 1805 in Milan. In the second half of the 18 c., another woman attracted the city's attention: Empress Maria-Theresa of Austria. In 1777, she had the grandiose royal palace of Piermarini built for her son Ferdinand, governor of Milan.

ABBAZIA DI MORIMONDO★

B2 *Piazza San Bernardo, 1 - Morimondo, 30 km to the south-west along the SS 494, towards Abbiategrasso - ℰ 02 94 96 19 19 - www.abbazia morimondo.it - church: Apr-Sept 8:30-12pm, 2:30pm-6prn (7pm on w/ends); Oct-Mar: 8:30-12pm, 2:30pm-4pm (5pm Sat and 6pm Sun); monastery: guided tours on w/ends 3pm-5:30pm (6 €).*

Begun in the 12C and consecrated in the late 13C. It has Lombard elements and a typically Cistercian structure (Latin cross shape, two aisles, apse facing eastwards and sober in the extreme). The interior is one of the first examples of the use of the pointed arch and has a 16C choir. In the right transept, a fresco of the *Madonna and Child with saint Bernard and saint Benedetto* is attributed to **Bernardino Luini.**

MONZA★

B2 *20 km north of Milan.*

Duomo★★

9am-12pm, 3pm-6pm. Built during the 13 and 14C at the site of the basilica erected by Theodelinda in the early 7C, it has an elegant **façade★★** (restored in the 19C by Luca Beltrami), by **Matteo da Campione**, one of the *Maestri campionesi* who promulgated the Lombard style in Italy. The **interior★**, rebuilt in the 17C, has lost all its original decoration, but contains sculpted masterpieces like the **stone pulpit★** by Matteo da Campione, serving as a console for the organ, the splendid silver gilt **altar-cloth★** (14C) and, in the right transept, the fresco *The tree of life* by **Arcimboldo**.

Cappella di Teodolinda★★ – *Left apse, guided visit by appt. at the museum - closed Sun am - 8 €.* The chapel is entirely covered with **frescoes★★**, made by the Zavattari brothers between 1441 and 1446, evoking the queen's life in 45 sumptuous and refined scenes. On the rear wall, a sarcophagus contains the corpse of

Theodelinda. The altar tabernacle contains the famous **iron crown★★**, a silverwork item probably made in the 8C. to hold one of the nails from the Cross of Christ.

Museo e Tesoro del Duomo★★

Via Lambro, sur le flanc gauche du duomo - ☎ 039 57 83 427 - www. museoduomomonza.it - 9am-6pm - closed Mon - museum 8 €, 14 € combined with chapel of Theodelinda. This magnificent museum traces the long history of the duomo through the artworks it houses. The most precious items are those given to the church by Theodelinda and her husband Agilulf when the building was founded in the 7C and those donated by King Bérenger in the early 10C. The beauty of the **silverwork items★★** from the 6-9C. is breathtaking: Agilulf's cross, Theodelinda's crown, the superb hen with chicks in sculpted silver. Just as astonishing: the diptych of Stilicone in ivory, the sapphire cup and the cross of the Realm or of Bérenger.

Reggia di Monza★

Viale Brianza, 1 - bus Z221 and Z208 from the center (Piazza Trento e Trieste) or a 20 min. walk from Piazza Duomo - ☎ 0392 31 55 36 - www. reggiadimonza.it - park: 7am-7pm (9:30pm in summer) - free; palace: 10am-7pm (10pm Fri) - closed Mon - 1st floor 12 €, 2nd and 3rd floors 10 €, combined ticket 19 €. Restaurant area with bistro, café and restaurant, gd. fl. The grandiose neo-classical edifice, built in 17777 by Piermarini for Ferdinand of Austria, was the favorite summer residence of the Kings of

Italy until the tragic **assassination of King Umberto I**st by the anarchist Gaetano Bresci, on 20 July 1900, just meters from the palace. The residence was then abandoned, its furniture emptied out and used for all manner of functions. The restoration of the immense building (over 600 rooms), undertaken in the 2000s, restored its former splendor.
1st floor: royal apartments★ – *Guided tour every 30 mins.* The rooms are decorated as they were in the 19th c. and have some of the original furniture. The visit incorporates the apartments of Margherita and King Umberto Ist, and the sumptuous ballroom with its Neoclassical decor.
2nd floor: private guest apartments – The rooms now house temporary exhibitions and still feature some of the original decoration.
3rd floor: belvedere – collections of Italian Design★ – From 1923 to 1927, the palace hosted exhibitions of Italien design that gave rise to the prestigious Triennale. In what was once the servants' rooms there is now a visitor route on the history of Italien design.
Parco di Monza★ – The pleasant grounds here contain a rose garden, a small theater and a chapel *(no entry for visitors)*. In the north of the immense park (688 ha) is the famous racing-track where Formula 1's **Monza Grand Prix** is held every year.

Certosa di Pavia

Via Del Monumento, 4 - ☎ 0382 92 56 13 - www.museo.certosadipavia. beniculturali.it - 9am-11:30am, 2:30pm-6pm (5pm Oct-Mar) - guided tours every 30 mins - leave a donation.

Interior, Duomo di Monza

An elaborate creation, the façade boasts a startling profuseness and richness of detail, while retaining an elegant sobriety in its structure. The lower and more ornate half was built between 1473 and 1499 by the **Mantegazza brothers**, and by the celebrated architect and sculptor **Amadeo**, who worked in Bergamo and elsewhere, and his pupil **Briosco**; the upper part was created by the architect and sculptor Cristoforo Lombardo, who finished its construction in 1560. There is infinite variety in the polychrome marble sculptures, medallions, statues of saints in niches, rinceau and garlands. Around the remarkable windows by Amadeo, note the scenes from the Bible, the life of Christ, and the life of Galeazzo Visconti. The bas-reliefs by Briosco around the central portal evoke episodes from the history of the Carthusians. Before entering the church, walk around it starting on the left-hand side, to admire the superb ensemble in the late Lombard Gothic style, with its superimposed galleries of arcades.

Interior and cloisters

With its solemn beauty, the interior is Gothic too, but there are signs of the forerunners of the Renaissance, particularly in the transept and choir. If you look up just after you enter, you'll see, beyond the left-hand chapels, a

Church façade, Certosa di Pavia

Carthusian (in trompe-l'œil) examining visitors through a gemeled window. Above it you can see *Eternal father* by **Perugino**.

In the right crosspiece is a *Madonna and Child* by **Bergognone** (1481-1522), who also created the *Madonna with rug*, above the entrance to the **small cloister**. On the ceiling of the **refectory**, adjoining the small cloister, is a *Madonna nursing*, also by Bergognone. Above the arcades of the **big cloister**, a vast and charming space, you can see the rooftops and chimneys of the **cells** in which, until 1968, the Carthusians lived: though sober in the extreme, each of them is an independent apartment, opening out on to a garden.

Going back into the church, you can admire, adorning the semi-dome vault above the right-hand altar in the transept, the **fresco** by Bergognone that shows the Virgin on a throne receiving from Galeazzo Visconti a replica of the chapter house. The duke's funerary monument dates from the late 15C.

The former **sacristy** contains a tryptych by **Baldassarre degli Embriachi** (late 14C) made from hippopatamus teeth and ivory. The left crosspiece also features work by Bergognone, with an *Ecce Homo*; it also houses the cenotaphe of Ludovico il Moro and Beatrice d'Este, sculpted by **Cristoforo Solari** (1497).

Bergamo★★★

The Upper Town and the Lower Town: two souls, two styles, two different perspectives on this charming town and its long history. Ruled successively by the Ligures, Gauls, Romans, Lombards, Venetians and Austrians before becoming Italian, Bergamo has a strong personality and an undeniable beauty, first glimpsed from afar, when its walls and monuments, often veiled in mist, appear almost all at once from Italy's busiest motorway.

▶ **Getting there:** Bergamo is 50km north-east of Milan, to which it is linked by the A4. The Upper Town is reserved for those coming by river and guests of the hotels. In the Lower Town, there are a number of well-signposted underground parking lots a few minutes' walk from the cable-car. A little farther out, you'll find the Piazzale Malpensata parking lot, behind the station. You can reach the city via the Città Alta cable-car, leaving from Corso Vittorio Emanuele II. You can travel here by train, from Milan's Stazione Centrale or the Stazione Garibaldi. There's a train every hour and the journey time is 50-70 mins.

City map p. 60. Map of Lombardy and the Lakes region (in the inside cover) B2.
▶ **Tip:** allow a full day.

CITTÀ ALTA★★★

In just a few minutes, the Città Alta cable-car passes through a tunnel carved out of the Venetian ramparts, to arrive at the picturesque **Piazza del Mercato delle Scarpe**, which you can also reach on foot by walking up the pretty **Via Pignolo★**.

Piazza Vecchia★★

A1 The political center of the city, this pretty square has a fountain given to Bergamo by the Doge of Venice Alvise Contarini in 1780. On the right, **Palazzo Scamozziano**, home to the municipal library and its 500,000 or so books, is in the Palladian style. Across from it is **Palazzo della Ragione**, which dates from 1199 but was rebuilt in the 16C.

Palazzo del Podestà – *A1*
☏ 035 24 71 16 - http://fondazione. bergamoestoria.it - every day except Mon 9:30am-1pm, 2:30pm-6pm - 5 €. This 12C palace contains the section of the History Museum of Bergamo dedicated to the Venetian period and the 16C. In the basement, the ruins of the Roman villa are displayed *(free entry)*.
Watching over the palace is the majestic **torre civica** *(elevator - same opening hours - 3 €)*, a 12th c. belfry with a 15C. clock. From the top there's a lovely **view★** of the historic city center.
The arcades of the Ragione palace connect it to Piazza del Duomo.

Piazza del Duomo★★

This charming square, the center of religious power, is a counterpart to Piazza Vecchia, the center of political power. The presence of two monumental churches in such a relatively small space is stunning: originally, the episcopal complex was composed of two buildings, San Vicenzo and Santa Maria Vetus. The latter was then replaced by Santa Maria Maggiore and became detached from the cathedral complex, and San Vicenzo became Bergamo's cathedral; it was dedicated to St. Alexander in 1689.

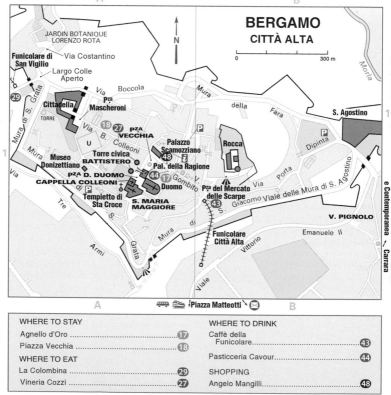

WHERE TO STAY		WHERE TO DRINK	
Agnello d'Oro	⑰	Caffè della Funicolare	㊸
Piazza Vecchia	⑱		
WHERE TO EAT		Pasticceria Cavour	㊹
La Colombina	㉙	SHOPPING	
Vineria Cozzi	㉗	Angelo Mangilli	㊽

Piazza Vecchia, Città Alta

61

Cappella Colleoni ★★★

A1 *Piazza Duomo - ☎ 035 21 00 61 - 9am-12:30pm, 2pm-4:30pm (2:30pm -6pm in summer) - closed Mon - free.*
The architect of the chapter house of Pavia, Amadeo, erected this jewel of the Lombard Renaissance between 1470 and 1476, to serve as a mausoleum for **Bartolomeo Colleoni** (1400-1475), Lord or Bergamo, the celebrated *condottiero* who lent his services to Milan and to the Republic of Venice. Built on the site of the sacristy of Santa Maria Maggiore, the funerary chapel is built into a recess in the basilica. The elegant **façade**, lined with precious polychrome marbles, is decorated in an exultant style,

embellished with fine sculptures and bas-reliefs that combine sacred and profane elements, as was the fashion in this era. The sumptuous **interior** is decorated with extraordinarily delicate sculptures, allegorical frescoes by **Tiepolo** and Renaissance **stalls** with marquetry. The **Colleoni monument**, by Amadeo, is surmounted with an equestrian statue of the *condottiero*, in gilded wood. The delicately chiselled bas-reliefs of the two tombs depicts scenes from the New Testament. In 1969, the remains of the *condottiero* were found, hidden beneath a false bottom. His favorite daughter, Medea, who died at the age of 15, lies in a tomb beside him *(left-hand wall)*, a marvel of delicate purity, also built by Amadeo.

Santa Maria Maggiore★★

A1 *Piazza Duomo - ℘ 035 21 13 55 - www.fondazionemia.it - 9am-12:30pm, 2:30pm-6pm (5pm in winter), Sun 9am-1pm, 3pm-6pm.*

The basilica dates from the 12C, but in the 14C Giovanni da Campione added two beautiful **porches★★** resting on lions, in the Lombard Roman style. The church has no main façade because it was part of the bishopric.

Interior – Redesigned in the Baroque style (late 16-early 17C), it is profusely decorated with stuccowork and gilt. The walls of the aisles and choir are cloaked with nine splendid Florentine **tapestries★★** (1580-1586), made on the basis of sketches by Alessandro Allori. On the rear wall of the nave, the sumptuous Flemish tapestry representing the **Crucifixion★★★** was woven in Anvers (1698). Above it, admire the grandiose depiction of the *Parting of the Red Sea* by **Luca Giordano** (1681). This part of the church also houses the tomb of **Donizetti** (1797-1848), made by the sculptor Vincenzo Vela (1820-1871). The interesting fresco of the *Tree of life* (1347) adorns the right tranSept Four superb **panels of marquetry★★** depicting the Old Testament are encased within the balustrade of the choir: they were made in the early 16th c. after sketches by **Lorenzo Lotto**. Exit the church into Piazza di Santa Maria Maggiore to admire the **south portal** (14C) and the charming **Cappella di Santa Croce**, quatrefoil in shape, built in around 1000 in the

primitive Roman style. It was part of the bishopric. Then go back into Piazza del Duomo by walking around the basilica and through the **chevet★**, whose apsidal chapels are adorned with arcades.

Battistero★

A1 Crowned with statues, the delightful octogonal baptistry, adorned with graciles colonnettes and statues (14C) representing the Virtues, is a reconstruction of the work by Giovanni da Campione (1340). Erected at the back of the nave of Santa Maria Maggiore but deemed too cumbersome, it was demolished in 1660 and rebuilt in 1898 in its current location.

Duomo

A1 *℘ 035 21 02 23 - 7:30am-11:45am, 3pm-6:30pm.*

The cathedral has a long history, one that you could scarcely guess at today, starting in the 5C. with the founding of a church dedicated to St. Vincent. The current edifice was built in 1459 by the architect Filarete and completed in the 19C. It contains interesting paintings by Giovan Battista Moroni, Sebastiano Ricci and Andrea Previtali. The wooden **choir** is a rich composition dating from 1698.

Museo e tesoro della Cattedrale – A2 *℘ 035 24 44 92 - www. fondazionebernareggi.it - every day except Mon 9:30am-1pm, 2pm-6:30pm - 5 €.* This very pleasant museum reveals the history of the cathedral, built on the site of ancient Roman *domus*. The digs unearthed an archaeological site that is now used as

---

Lorenzo Lotto: a Venetian in Bergamo

The Venetian painter Lorenzo Lotto (1480-1556) was summoned to Bergamo in 1513 by the Dominicans. He stayed there until 1525. His œuvre, influenced by Bellini, Raphael and Dürer, is marked by the tenderness and unease evinced by the characters. Several churches in the Lower Town house some fine examples. His key work, however, an admirable cycle of frescoes★ illustrating the lives of saints Barbara and Brigitte, is housed at the Oratorio Suardi in Trescore Balneario. 13 km east of Bergamo via the S 42 - guided tours Mar-Nov Sun 3pm and by reservation on other days at Pro Loco de Trescore, via Suardi, 20 - ℘ 035 94 47 77 - www.prolocotrescore.it.

---

the backdrop for an exhibition of items from the treasury (liturgical crosses, textiles, icons etc.).

From Piazza Vecchia, head down Via Bartolomeo Colleoni to reach the **Cittadella**, built by the Viscontis in 1355.

Beyond the fortifications, you can take the funicular to the ruins of the castle of **San Vigilio** where there is a **panoramic view★** of the plain and the city.

CITTÀ BASSA★

From a tourist's perspective, the Lower Town is somewhat overshadowed by the breathtaking Upper Town, but this is a pity as it offers some very nice walks and the must-see Accademia Carrara. While the Upper Town contained the political and religious centers, the Lower Town was Bergamo's commercial center, a role it still plays today.

Largo Gavazzeni (Piazza Matteotti)

The immense square, the heart of the rationalist city designed by **Marcello Piacentini, Giovanni Muzio** and **Luigi Angelini** between 1920 and 1930, was renamed in honor of the conductor and composer from Bergamo: Gianandrea Gavazzeni (1909-1996). Beside it is the **Sentierone**, a promenade opened in the 17C by the city's merchants. On the square is the **Donizetti theater** (1786-1898) and the **San Bartolomeo** church, home to the magnificent **Martinengo Altarpiece★** by Lorenzo Lotto, depicting the Virgin on a throne, surrounded by saints. Leading off from the Sentierone is **Via XX Settembre**, which, along with the pretty **Via Sant'Alessandro** and **Via Sant'Orsola** forms the commercial heart of the city.

Old district★

This district extends around **Via Pignolo★**, sinuous and lined with former palaces from the 16C and 18C, and churches filled with artworks, including **San Bernardino**, where, above the altar, there is a splendid **Madonna and Child enthroned with saints★** painted by **Lorenzo Lotto** in 1521 (note the color values, with the combination of the bright red of the Madonna's robe and the intense green of the drape held by the angels). As for the **Santo Spirito** church, it has a

63

St. John the Baptist with saints and
a polyptych by Previtali, a polyptych
representing the Madonna by
Bergognone, and a *Madonna and Child*
by **Lorenzo Lotto**.

Accademia Carrara★★★
*Piazza Giacomo Carrara, 82 - ℘ 035
23 43 96 - www.accademiacarrara.
bergamo.it - every day except Tue
10am-7pm - 10 €. Allow 2hrs.*
Founded in 1796, the Accademia
occupies a neo-classical palace built
in 1810. The wonderful collections are
among the most important in Italy
and benefit from a restored setting.
Visitors can see 28 rooms spread over
2 floors, following a route that is both
chronological (15-19C) and thematic,
clear and very plesant. The most
prestigious section is that of the Italian
schools of the 15-17C., incorporating
works by Botticelli, Pisanello, Giovanni
Bellini, Andrea Mantegna, Carpaccio,
Lorenzo Lotto and Raphael.
1st floor – Houses chefs-d'œuvre like
the magnificent *Madonna and Child*
and the *San Bernardino* by **Andrea
Mantegna**, the portrait of Lionel d'Este,
elegant and refined, by **Pisanello**;
two very different types of *Madonna
and Child,* one by **Carlo Crivelli**, still
Gothic in the gold of the Virgin's
cloak, and the other by **Cosimo Tura**,
a master from the Ferrara school,
with heightened realism and angular
shapes influenced by Flemish art.
In the section on Venetian art, note
the magnificent *Madonna di Alzano*

by **Giovanni Bellini**. In room 4, we
move on to the Tuscan and Umbrian
Renaissance: portrait of Giuliano de'
Medici, with a stern profile, *Christ
giving the blessing* and *The Story of
Virginia* by **Botticelli**; *Saint Sebastian*,
a work of magesterial finesse in its
execution by **Raphael**.
2nd floor – Rooms 14 and 15 are
dedicated to the Venetian **Lorenzo
Lotto**: the melancholic *Portrait of
a young man*, the splendid *Mystic
Marriage of St. Catherine,* the *Holy
Family with St. Catherine* and the
Portrait of Lucina Brembate. After
room 16, dedicated to 16C Venetian
painting (*Madonna and Child* by
Titian), we move on to portraits by
the Bergamese **Giovanni Battista
Moroni** (room 17) and works by the
Dutchman Matthias Stomer influenced
by Caravaggio (room 19). In the
section on 'genre' painting (room
23), the quirky still lifes with musical
instruments by the Bergamase
Evaristo Baschenis (1617-1667) deserve
a mention: note the detail of the dust
on the instruments, symbolizing the
passing of time.
After the portraits in room 26 (**Piccio**,
Portrait of Countess Anastasia Spini),
we arrive at the historic painting
that triumphs in the 19C. (**Francesco
Hayez**, *Caterina Cornaro*, room 27). A
different kind of intensity and intimacy
altogether is seen in *Memory of Grief*
by **Giuseppe Pellizza da Volpedo**
(room 28).

Lake Maggiore★★★

Embedded like a jewel in the snow-topped Alps, Lake Maggiore, with its sapphire waters, is a place for superlatives. It may not be Italy's biggest lake (that's Lake Garda), but its gentle climate, abundant flora and sumptuous landscapes have long seduced the rich and powerful, who have had castles and villas built here, amid immense gardens with terraces. The villages that line its shores, sparkling holiday destinations shaded by palm trees and magnolias, afford a unique view panorama over the lake; the Borromean Islands take refinement and aesthetics to new heights.

▶**Getting there:** The shores of the lake can be reached via the A8 and also by bus or train. See p. 123.

Map p. 67. Map of Lombardy and the Lakes region (inside the cover) A2.
▶**Tip:** Try to visit the region in April-May, when the camellias and rhododendrons are in bloom. To visit the Borromean Islands—accessible from the western shore from Stresa, Carciano, Baveno or Pallanza—allow a full day and get hold of a timetable for the boat rides, so you can plan your trips between the islands. The **Lago Maggiore Express** (👆 *see p. 128*) Offers package deals that let you discover the lake and surrounding country.

EASTERN SHORE★

With nature at the forefront north of Laveno, and culture taking its place farther south, the lake's eastern shore, far less exposed than the western one, is also considerably less touristy.

Angera★
65 km north-east of Milan.
The hulking **Rocca Borromeo** dominates this small town to the south of Lake Maggiore, offering a lovely view of the lake and islands. Inside, in the Justice room, some remarkable 14C **frescoes**★★ celebrate the life of the archbishop Ottone Visconti. The fortress also houses the **Museo della Bambola e del Gioco**★ (museum of

Puppets and Toys), where there is lots to see. *☎ 0331 93 13 00 - www. isoleborromee.it - late Mar-late Oct: 9am-5:30pm.*

Santa Caterina del Sasso★
Near Leggiuno, approx. 15 km north of Angera. Boat from Stresa: Apr-Sept - www.navigazionelaghi.it - from the lake, access via a staircase with 80 steps; parking spaces on the road, descend via a staircase with 240 steps or an elevator (0.50 €). ☎ 0332 64 71 72 - www. santacaterinadelsasso.com - 9am-12pm, 2pm-6pm (5pm in winter); in Nov-Feb w/end only - leave an offering.
Clinging to the cliff that overlooks the lake, the hermitage founded by the

> ### The Borromeo family
> *Originally from Tuscany, the Borromeo family were exiled from there in the 14th c. after opposing Florence. Skilled merchants and bankers, they accrued a colossal fortune, enabling them to buy land in Lombardy and form alliances with the other great families of the region, the Viscontis and the Sforzas. Several Borromeos were also princes of the Church, including St. Charles Borromeo. Today, two family members often appear in the world's gossip columns: Lavinia Borromeo, the wife of the president of FIAT John Elkann, and Beatrice Borromeo, wife of the prince of Monaco Pierre Casiraghi.*

anchorite Alberto Besozzo in the 13C. overhangs the lake, at a magnificent **site★**.

The chapter house and church house frescoes dating from the 14-18C.

Cerro★

This tranquil village has a tiny fishing port whose banks are shaded by the **Museo Internazionale Design Ceramico**, dedicated to ceramic artworks. *Via Lungolago Perabò, 5 - ℘ 0332 62 55 110 - www.midec.org - 10am-12:30pm, 2:30pm-5:30pm - closed Mon and Tue afternoons.*

Laveno Mombello

This big, peaceful market town is the departure point for the ferries that go to Verbania-Intra.

North of the village, a cableway leads to the top of **Sasso del Ferro★★** (1,100m), a meeting point for paragliders, where there's a vast **panorama** over the entire region. *℘ 0332 668 012 - www.funiviedellagomaggiore.it - Apr-Oct 11am-6:30pm; rest of the year w/end only - 10 € AR.*

Porta Bozzolo

À Casalzuigno, 8 km à l'est de Laveno Mombello - ℘ 0322 62 41 36 - www.visitfai.it/villadellaportabozzolo/- 10am-6pm (5pm Oct-Nov) - closed Mon, Tue and Dec-Feb - 8.50 €.

The villa, built in the 16C, was transformed in the next century into a 'villa of delights' with a prettily decorated interior. Beside it is a scenic **parc★**, on the sheer hillside.

Luino

The largest town on the eastern shore, it is not lacking in charm, particularly on Wednesdays, the main market day. Close to the Swiss border (*9km*), the market town of **Maccagno** is home to the interesting **Parisi Valle Museum of Contemporary Art** (*www.museoparisivalle.it*), in a building that forms a bridge over the river Giona and is the sanctuary of the **Madonna della Punta** which dominates the lake.

WESTERN SHORE★★★

The western shore of the lake, which gets the most sunshine, is where most of the main places of interest are to be found.

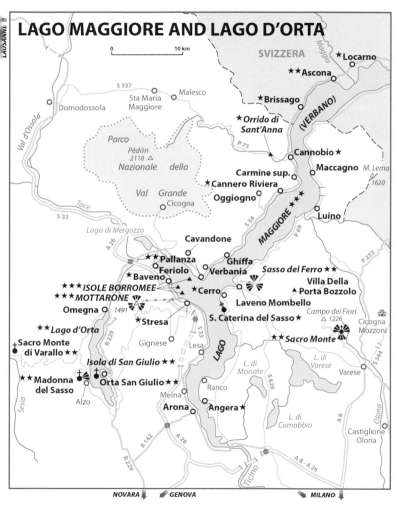

LAGO MAGGIORE AND LAGO D'ORTA

0 ⊢————————⊣ 10 km

LAUSANNE

SVIZZERA

★ **Locarno**

★★ **Ascona**

★ **Brissago**

Malesco

Sta Maria
Maggiore

Domodossola

Maggia

(VERBANO)

★ *Orrido di
Sant'Anna*

P 75

Cannobio ★

Maccagno M. Lema
1620

Parco
Pédún
2110 △
Nazionale della
Val Grande
Cicogna

Carmine sup.
★ **Cannero Riviera**
Oggiogno ○

Val d'Ossola

Toce

S 33

Lago di Mergozzo

A 26

★★★

MAGGIORE

P 69

Luino

Cavandone

★★ **Pallanza**
★ **Feriolo**
★ **Baveno**
★★★ *ISOLE BORROMEE*
★★★ *MOTTARONE*
Omegna ○ 1491

Ghiffa
Verbania
★ **Cerro**

Sasso del Ferro ★★

Villa Della
● **Porta Bozzolo**

Campo dei Fiori
△ 1226

Cicogna
Mozzoni

Laveno Mombello

★★ *Lago d'Orta*
★ **Sacro Monte
di Varallo** ★★

★ **Stresa**

Gignese

S. Caterina del Sasso ★

★★ *Sacro Monte*

Isola di San Giulio ★★

Lesa

LAGO

*L. di
Monate*

*L. di
Varese*

Varese

★★ **Madonna
del Sasso**

Orta San Giulio ★★

Alzo

R 229

Meina

Arona ○

Ranco

S 629

Angera ★

*L. di
Comabbio*

Castiglione
Olona

Olona

A 8

R 142

A 26

Sesia

Ticino

A 8 - A 26

67

NOVARA ▥   ⬦ GENOVA   ⬦ MILANO ▥

Tickets for the Borromean Islands

There are many types of tickets (👆 see www.isoleborromee.it): Isola Bella - 16 €; Isola Madre - 13€; Isola Bella + Isola Madre - 21 €; Rocca di Angera - 9.50 €; Isola Bella + Isola Madre + Rocca di Angera - 25 €; Villa Pallavicino - 9.50 €; Isola Bella + Villa Pallavicino - 18 €; Isola Madre + Villa Pallavicino - 16 €; Rocca di Angera + Villa Pallavicino - 12 €; Isola Bella + Isola Madre + Villa Pallavicino - 25 €; Isola Bella + Isola Madre + Rocca di Angera + Villa Pallavicino - 31 €.

Arona

70km north-west of Milan.

This commercial town, though not of great interest to tourists, offers a pleasant walk beside the lake and, from the ruins of its citadel, a gorgeous **view**★ of the Rocca at Angera. The monumental bronze **statue**★ by San Carlone (1698) rises some 24 m high at the town's northern exit. It represents Charles Borromeo, the cardinal and archbishop of Milan, celebrated for the courage he showed during the plague of 1576. An internal staircase leads up to the windows, from which there's a great view. *Apr-Sep: 9am-12:30pm, 2pm-6:30pm; Oct-Dec and Mar: w/end 9am-12:30pm, 2pm-4:30pm (Sun only in Dec) - closed Jan-Feb - 6 €.*

Stresa★

18 km north of Arona.

This serene holiday resort with its attractive Liberty villas is one of the most popular areas on the lake's shores. The market town stretches all along the lake to the north, where there is a row of palaces from the 1900s. Take a stroll to reach an observation point looking out at the Borromean Islands.

Villa Pallavicino★ – *📞 0323 31 533 - www.parcozoopallavicino.it - mid-Mar to late Oct: 9am-7pm - see inset above. Little train leaving from the jetty at Stresa: 9:30am-4:30pm - 4 €.* At the entrance to the town, there is an animal park and botanical garden in a space of 20 hectares, fully signposted and great for children.

Borromean Islands★★★

Get here from the ferry terminals at Stresa, Carciano, Baveno or Pallanza - www.navigazionelaghi.it - ticket for unlimited travel between the three islands, leaving from Stresa 16.90 €. 📞 0323 30 556 - www.isoleborromee.it - visits: late Mar to late Oct: 9am-5:30pm - see box above - allow almost a full day.

These three islets across from Stresa are named for the princely Borromeo family, who lived here from the 15C. onwards and still own the land today. **Isola Bella** – This islet, much-loved by tourists, is taken up entirely by the **palace** built by Charles III Borromeo (1586-1652) and redesigned by his son Vitaliano VI (1620-1690). The isle was named in honor of Isabella, the wife of Charles III. The palace, where Napoleon once stayed in 1797, hosted the **Stresa conference** in 1935, bringing together

Isola Bella, Lake Maggiore

Mussolini and the British and French representatives. The three countries had reached an agreement on opposing the re-arming of Germany, but Hitler's support for Italy's conquest of Ethiopia in the same year prompted Italy to switch over to the German side. After the state rooms, which alternate between the Baroque style and classical patterns, you visit the 'piano nobile' with the ravishing **Galleria Berthier** *(9am-1pm, 2pm-5pm - 3 €)*, housing chefs-d'œuvre from the Lombard Baroque period and the sumptuous Throne Room and Queens' Room. The visitor route leads to the **grottoes**, where a rockery and seashells evoke the ocean depths. The **gardens**, laid out in a stepped pattern and peopled with statues inspired by mythology, are akin to a theater set design. At the top, the 'amphitheater', shaped like a shell, is extraordinarily scenic.

Isola dei Pescatori – Situated between the other two islands, this one has managed, despite being invaded by restaurants and touristy shops, to retain the look of a fishing village. It affords visitors an unrivalled view of Isola Bella, the lake and the surrounding mountains. Tucked away in its little streets is a pretty church dedicated to San Vittore.

Isola Madre – This islet, the one farthest from Stresa and the largest in the archipelago, is also the most secretive. It is entirely taken up by an 8 ha **garden** composed of plants brought back from five continents since the 19C, with peacocks, parrots and pheasants roaming among them. The palace houses a remarkable **puppet theater** (17-19C) of the house of Borromeo, which presents, among other shows, the intriguing 'Theater of Hell'.

Mottarone★★★

The road from Mottarone *(a toll road)* leads through wooded parkland to the summit of the mountain (1491 m), from where there is a magnificent **panorama★★★** over the region's lakes, the Alps and the Monte Rosa Massif. You can also get to the summit via the **cableway** *(funivia)* which is next to the Carciano jetty. *If you're planning to make the ascent after visiting the Borromean Islands, get off at Carciano. ℘ 0323 30 295 - www.stresa-mottarone.it; Apr-Oct 9:30am-5:30pm, winter 9:10am-4:50pm - 19 €.*
Halfway up, the **Giardino botanico Alpinia** contains 1,000 species of coastal plain plants and high elevation plants from the alpine mountain range, as well as some Asian varieties. *Get there via the funicular, midway station. ℘ 032 330 295 - Apr-Oct 9:30am-6pm - 3 €.*
From the summit of Mottarone, you can continue your tour of Lake Maggiore, or go down to Lake Orta (*see p. 73*) via a road that offers pleasant views of the lake *(approx. 20km to Orta).*

Baveno★

5 km north of Stresa.
This attractive holiday resort acquired some sumptuous residences in the 19C At its center, the 5C **baptistry** is adorned with Renaissance frescoes and stands beside a Roman church, in a lovely juxtaposition of styles. Continuing northwards, you reach the charming market town of **Feriolo**. On its attractive promenade, you can enjoy live music at the cafés in the summer.

Verbania

10 km east of Baveno. Approximately 4 km separate the districts of Intra and Pallanza (bus every 40 mins).
The biggest town in the Lake Maggiore area contains multiple *frazioni* (villages), including **Suna**, **Pallanza** and **Intra**. Tranquil Pallanza has the greatest appeal, while Intra has the look of a modern and active town. Cars come here to board the ferry to Laveno, on the Lombard shore.
Pallanza★★ – This pleasant holiday destination has a nice assortment of cafés and restaurants. If you head upwards during a walk or bike-ride, you'll be able to see the lush vegetation that surrounds the town, embellished in spring with the pink and red hues of camellias and rhododendrons.
In the heart of the district, the lovely Roman church, **Madonna di Campagna**, has an octagonal cupola with arcades and small columns. Step inside to discover frescoes from the 15th c. (Nursing Madonna) and 16th c. (musician-angel). The **Museo del**

Paesaggio has an interesting section on the casts of **Paul Troubetzkoy** (born in Intra in 1866), an ample collection of landscapes by 19 and 20C artists and sculptures by Arturo Martini. *Via Ruga, 44 - ☏ 0323 55 66 21 - www.museodelpaesaggio.it - Fri 2pm-5pm, w/end 11am-5pm -5 €.*

Villa Giulia opens onto a pleasant public garden, with a little cafeteria with terrace across from the lake and the snowy peaks of the Swiss border. *Via Vittorio Veneto - 9am-6pm.* For a nice walk (*1hr 30*) or bike-ride, walk beside the lake along Via Troubetzkoy, to the south, as far as Via Buon Rimedio. A diagonal route through the woods leads to the village of **Cavandone** *(map available at the tourist office).*

Villa Taranto★★ – *☏ 0323 40 45 55 - www.villataranto.it - Mar-Oct: 8:30am-6:30pm (4pm in Oct) - 10 €. You can also get to the gardens by boat; get off at Villa Taranto.* Situated at the exit from the town, on the Intra road, the villa was bought in the 1930s by captain Neil McEacharn, who rechristened it in honor of his ancestor Jacques MacDonald, made Duke of Tarento by Napoleon. Marrying French, Italian and English styles, its magnificent **gardens,** spread among terraces and featuring fountains and pools with water lilies, is home to 20,000 species of flora. A delight for the eyes and the nostrils.

Sacro Monte di Ghiffa

Approx. 6 km north of Verbania via the SS 34. ☏ 0323 59 870 - www. sacromonte-ghiffa.com - 8am-4:30pm. Above the village of Ghiffa, in the mountains, is a series of Baroque chapels whose surrounding environment, classed as a nature reserve, has been endowed with picnic areas and nature trails.

An **archaeological trail** shows you rocks bearing neolithic engravings and a **observation point** overlooking Lake Maggiore.

At **Ghiffa**, the compact **Museo dell'Arte del Cappello** tells the story of the hats made by the famous Panizza factory. *Corso Belvedere, 279 - ☏ 0323 59 209 - www.museodellartedelcappello.it - Apr-Oct: w/end 3:30pm-6:30pm; Jul-Aug also Mar and Thurs - 1.50 €.*

Cannero Riviera★

15 km north of Verbania. Clinging to the slopes of Monte Carza, this pretty climate station stacks its houses above the lake, among the olive trees, vines, orange and lemon trees, palm trees and camellias. From the shore, flanked by a lovely promenade lined with magnolias, you can see the islets on which the ruins of the **castles of Malpaga** (14C). The footpath to **Oggiogno**, 515 m long, offers impressive views of the lake. *2 hrs' easy walking. You can take one of several walks from there to the surrounding villages (more info available at the tourist office).* Halfway between Cannero Riviera and Cannobio, look out for the signpost for **Carmine Superiore**, so that you don't miss this picturesque medieval market town, dominated by the clocktower of the San Gottardo church (14C), which has frescoes from the 15C.

Cannobio★

8 km north of Cannero Riviera.
The proximity of the Swiss border (*5 km to the north*) can be detected in the architecture of this village, whose commercial upper part contains the **Palazzo della Ragione** (13C), a former town hall that hosts exhibitions.
In the lower part, the important Renaissance sanctuary of the **Madonna della Pietà** has Baroque decor and a 16C altarpiece.
Farther up the river, the **Orrido di Sant'Anna★** forms an impressive gorge, lined with high schist cliffs.

Ascona★★ (Switzerland)

A former fishing village, that became Lake Maggiore's answer to St. Tropez from the 1950s onwards, Ascona has an elegant promenade flanked by the terraces of cafés and restaurants. In the heart of the market town is the **Santi Pietro e Paolo** church, with works by Giovanni Serodine (1594-1630), born in Ascona and taught by Caravaggio, and the interesting **Museo Comunale di Arte Moderna**. *Closed for renovation work at the time of writing. Via Borgo, 34 - ℘ +41 (0)91 759 81 40 - www.museoascona.ch.*
Near the town center, the **Santa Maria della Misericordia★** church (14-15C) houses fascinating 15-16C frescoes and a fine altarpiece for the main altar, from 1519. A 10-min. walk from the center, the **Museo Castello San Materno★** has works by German impressionist artists (Max Lieberman), the Die Brücke movement (Ernst Ludwig Kirchner, Emil Nolde) and the Blaue Reiter (Alexej von Jawlensky,

August Macke). *Via Losone 10 - ℘ +41 (0)91 759 81 60 - http:// museoascona.ch.*
Monte Verità★ – *Strada Collina, 84 - ℘ 091 785 40 40 - www. monteverita.org.* In the early 20C the wood-lined hill that dominates the village was home to a community of artists, psychoanalysts and anarchists seeking a new way of life. The site now houses a cultural center, a hotel, a restaurant and a museum that tells the story of this exciting period.

Brissago Islands★ (Switzerland)

Get there by boat from Brissago, Ascona and Locarno, www. navigazionelaghi.it. ℘ 091 791 43 61 - www.isolebrissago.ch - late Mar to late Oct: 9am-6pm - 8 CHF.
The islands, home to the **Botanical garden of the Canton of Tessin**, were acquired in 1885 by the Baron of Saint-Léger who turned them into an enchanting exotic garden.

Locarno★ (Switzerland)

Ensconced in a sun-kissed cove, Locarno is blessed with a lovely climate. In August, lovely **Piazza Grande★**, lined with Lombard-style arcades, hosts the International Film Festival and becomes a magnificent outdoor movie theater. The gardens, the shores of the lank, the peaks of **Cimetta★★** (1350 m), the sanctuary of the **Madonna del Sasso★★** (15-17C) at Orsellina (*access by funicular, from Via della Stazione*) and the hillsides covered with vines provide ample incentive for a stroll.

Lake Orta★★

With its very mild climate, Lake Orta, separated from Lake Maggiore by Mt. Mottarone, is one of the smallest Lombard lakes but also one of the most graceful, with its wood-lined banks and the tiny isle of San Giulio. Less busy than the other lakes, Lake Orta retains the charm of destinations off the beaten track, while the Sacred Mount, a UNESCO world heritage site, boasts woodland interspersed with Baroque chapels.

▶**Getting there:** The A26 goes to the lake, and there's a bus from Stresa.
⏱ *See p. 123.*
Map p. 67. Map of Lombardy and the Lakes region (inside cover) A2.
▶**Tip:** Instead of getting here via the main roads (SS 229), take the far more scenic mountain road, which leaves from Stresa and goes via Gignese and Armeno (approx. 40km).

ORTA SAN GIULIO★★

Located on a peninsula that protrudes into the southern half of the lake, this ravishing village, reached via sheer roads and stairs, stretches its little streets lined with old houses along the shore of the lake. On arrival, a sort of minaret marks the location of **Villa Crespi**, a magnificent Moorish-style building dating from 1879, which houses a well-known restaurant. Opposite the disembarking point, the **Palazzotto★**, the 16C. former communal palace, is adorned with frescoes and houses temporary exhibitions.

ISOLA DI SAN GIULIO★★

Boat trips here from Orta every 10 mins - ☎ 333 605 02 88 - www. motoscafisti.com. No entry during services, celebrated with Gregorian chants. Private water-taxis on request.

It's at night, from the village, that you get the best view of the island. Artistic lighting makes it seem almost otherworldly. The **basilica di San Giulio** dominates this island that measures just 300m by 160m. It was supposedly founded by St. Julius in the 4C. Inside, there's a remarkable 12C. **ambon★** (pulpit) in black serpentine, adorned with symbols of the apostles, and some fine **frescoes** from the school of Gaudenzio Ferrari (16C). In the crypt, a shrine contains the remains of St. Julius.

SACRO MONTE D'ORTA★

1.5 km from Orta San Giulio. Get here via the little train.
Perched atop a hill overlooking the lake, at a site classed as a nature reserve, this Sacred Mountain has twenty **Baroque chapels** (16-17C) dedicated to St. Francis of Assisi. They are all decorated with frescoes and

> ### The Sacred Mountains
>
> A UNESCO heritage site since 2003, the Sacred Mountains of North Italy—seven in Piedmont and two in Lombardy—were built from the 15C in order to provide an alternative place of prayer to those of Jerusalem and Palestine, which were difficult to reach. The Franciscans, guardians of the Church of the Holy Sepulcher, selected the sites, including Varallo, which belonged to the Duchy of Milan, to build 'new Jerusalems' there. After the Council of Trentino in 1545, this model was used above all in the dioceses of Milan to combat the influence of Protestant Reforms. This encouraged the creation of other sacred mountains, dedicated not only to Christ, but also to the cult of the Virgin Mary, the saints, the Trinity and the Rosary. This project was greatly supported by Charles Borromeo, bishop of Milan. Their integration into the natural landscapes is particularly remarkable, as are the artworks that they house, particularly those of Gaudenzio Ferrari (1840-1545), influenced by Leonardo da Vinci.
>
> In the lakes region, there is also the **Sacro Monte di Varese**★★ (8km north-west of the city with the same name), composed of 14 chapels from the 17C, adorned with frescoes with trompe-l'œil and terracotta sculptures. Magnificent **view**★★ of the lakes, too.

74

populated with polychrome terracotta characters evoking episodes from the life of the saint, in a style that is at once realistic and theatrical.

Head round the southern tip of the lake until you get to Alzo, from where you climb up to the sanctuary of the **Madonna del Sasso**. From the terrace of the 18C church, enjoy a magnificent **view**★★ of the lake embedded in its jewelry-box of green mountains.

❯ *Return to Alzo and head to Varallo, twenty kilometers to the west.*

Varallo, the industrial and commercial hub of the Sesia valley, is known for the pilgrimage to the Sacro Monte.

SACRO MONTE DI VARALLO★★

Access by car (parking lot) or funicular (9am-5pm, 6pm in summer) - ☏ 0163 53 938 - www.sacromonte-varallo.com - allow 3hrs for the visit.

Situated in a vast wood-lined park that dominates the town, this astonishing ensemble came into being in the 15C. The site, dubbed 'The New Jerusalem', houses a grotto of Bethlehem, the Virgin's tomb, Golgotha. In the 16C, it was decided that major episodes from the life of Christ should be added to the site.

Around the **Baroque church**★, a total of **43 chapels**★★★ (16-18C) were therefore built, all brought to life by hundreds of highly evocative frescoes and sculptures, created by multiple artists, including the painter **Gaudenzio Ferrari**.

Head back to the lake.

To complete your tour of the lake, climb back towards the northern tip to **Omegna**, birthplace of **Gianni Rodari** (1920-80), the famous poet and author of books for children.

Lake Como★★★

Dominated by the snowy peaks of the Alps almost all year round, Lake Como, also known as Lario, elegantly blends nature and art. On its shores, cypress trees, olive trees and palm trees mingle with rhododendron bushes and azaleas, in a harmonious marriage of Mediterranean and more temperate essences. Seduced by the magic of the area, 19C aesthetes and philanthropists from the installed sumptuous collections of painting and sculptures in their villas, amid the terraces of their Italian or English-style gardens. Now popular with the international jet-setting class, the pretty villages sprawl across the embankment or cling to the hillside. With its sheer drops and tunnels, the road that circles the lake offers unparalleled views. Of the three branches, the promontory of Bellagio is its most attractive part.

▶**Getting there:** Como can be reached via the A8 and by train (the station is across from the lake and the ferry terminals, accessible from the station Milano Cadorna). & *See p. 123*.
Map p. 76. Map of Lombardy and the Lakes region (inside cover) B1-2.
▶**Tip:** Allow two days. To take full advantage of the scenery and admire the villas, go by bus and come back by boat. To visit the eastern shore, it's best to take the ferry to Bellagio to get to Varenna, then continue by car to the Abbazia di Piona.

COMO★

An important commercial and industrial center, Como bears no traces of the ancient Roman city whose birth the erudite Pliny the Younger and Pliny the Elder witnessed; the Milanese, who destroyed it in 1127, nonetheless copied the know-how of the '*maestri comacini*', the masons-architects-sculptors who took the Lombard style to all parts of Europe, and the weavers, who taught the art of working with **silk** from the Middle Ages onwards. In the 1930s, Como was used as an experimentation ground for architects skilled at architectural rationalism. The **Novocomum** (*Via Giuseppe Sinigaglia, 1*) and the former **Casa del Fascio** (*Piazza Verdi, in front of the apse of the duomo*), by Giuseppe Terragni, are the most significant examples of this movement, which advocated the use of new materials (reinforced concrete, vast glazed surfaces).

Historic center
Duomo★★ – *7am-12pm, 3pm-7pm.* There's a mixture of Gothic, Renaissance and classical styles; the architect Filippo Juvarra added a Baroque touch in the 18C by giving it a large octagonal cupola. The decor of the **façade★★** (1484) abounds with tiny, finely-crafted statues that are

only matched by the sculptures on the north portal (16C.), known as 'della Rana': a frog (*rana*) can indeed be seen on one of the pilasters.

The **interior★** has some beautiful 16 and 17C **tapestries★**, paintings by B. Luini (*Adoration of the Magi*, **Madonna and child with the saints★**) and G. Ferrari (*Marriage of the Virgin*), and a remarkable **altarpiece★** in gilded wood dedicated to St. Abbondio (16C). Welded to the façade of the Duomo, the **Broletto★★**, topped with the Clocktower, is the 13C former communal palace.

If you walk up Via Vittorio Emanuele II, the main commercial artery, you get to Piazza San Fedele, a former Roman forum where, among the medieval maisonettes and arcades, is the **San Fedele★**, a basilica in the Roman Lombard style (12C) with portals covered with sculptures. Splendid **choir★** inside.

Tempio Voltiano (temple of Volta) – *Viale Marconi - ℘ 031 57 47 05 - http:// cultura.comune.como.it/tempio-voltiano/ - 9:30am-6pm - closed Mon - 4 €.* Erected near the lake and the monument to the dead, this small neo-classical edifice celebrates the memory of the polymath **Alessandro Volta** (1745-1827), born in Como, who invented the electric battery and who gave the volt its name.

Around the center

Basilica di Sant'Abbondio★ –
Approx. 1km south-west of Como. Chef-d'œuvre of Roman Lombard architecture (11C), it has two square clocktowers. Its **façade★** is preceded by a beautiful portal.

Inside, there are remarkable 14C **frescoes★** tracing the life of Christ in a range of red and beige hues.

Villa Olmo – *3 km to the north, via the S 35, then to the right via the S 340. Via Cantoni, 1 - ℘ 031 24 25 43 - www.grandimostrecomo.it/villa-olmo - gardens: summer 8am-11pm; winter: 9am-7pm - free.* A majestic Neoclassical edifice now used as a venue for exhibitions, this villa stands on the southern shore of the lake. The gardens around it afford visitors a lovely **view★** of Como and the lake.

To learn about the craft of silk-working, go to the **Museo didattico della Seta** (*Silk Museum*). *Via Castelnuovo, 9, take the road to Varese and follow the signs - ℘ 031 30 31 80 - www.museosetacomo.com - 10am-6pm, Sat 10am-1pm - closed Sun-Mon - 10 €.*

To enjoy a splendid **panorama★** of the lake and the town, take the **funicular** up to **Brunate**, a village perched on the north-east tip of Como. There are several signposted walks that start there. *Piazza Alcide de Gasperi, 4 - ℘ 031 30 36 08 - www.funicolare como.it - every day 6am-10:30pm (Sat 12am) - 5.50 €.*

WESTERN SHORE★★

Cernobbio★★
4km north of Como.

The jet-set flock to this major resort beside the lake and stay at **Villa d'Este**, a superb Renaissance building converted into a securely guarded luxury hotel.

From Piazza del Risorgimento, near the jetty, there's a nice view of the lake. Strada Regina goes through some pretty villages like **Moltrasio**, **Laglio** and **Brienno**.

Ossuccio

The village is home to an interesting Roman church dedicated to the saints Giacomo and Filippo, with a bell-tower open to the elements at the sides and some 11C frescoes.

As for the Santa Maria Maddalena church (12C), it has a distinctive bell-tower that has become one of the symbols of the lake.

Near the church, the former medieval hospice houses an antiquarium. Upstream of the town is the sacred mountain of the **Madonna del Soccorso** (17-18C).

Isola Comacina★

Get here from the antiquarium in Ossuccio by water-taxi or by regular boat from Sala Comacina, Lenno and Tremezzo. ℘ 0344 56 369 - www. isola-comacina.it - mid-Mar to mid-Oct 10am-5pm (Jul-Aug 6pm) - 6 € excl. transportation.

This wooded isle is thought to have been an important cultural center in Antiquity, as the ruins found here suggest. It then served as a refuge for Christians fleeing the Barbarian invasions; various legends, including that of the Holy Grail, are connected to this peaceful place that is now a haven for artists. On St. John's Day, fireworks light up the sky here.

Villa del Balbianello★★

You can get here via the path from the church of Lenno (1 km), or by boat from Lenno (7.50 €). ℘ 0344 56 110 - www. visitfai.it/villadelbalbianello - mid-Mar to mid-Nov: 10am-6pm - closed Mon and Wed - gardens 10 €, combined ticket for gardens & villa (guided visit) 20 €.

At the end of the promontory that rises like a watchtower over the lake, the villa stands among cypresses and citrons in an enchanting setting. This 18C residence was owned by a cardinal, then by the Arconati Visconti family and, later, Guido Monzino (1928-88), a wealthy entrepreneur with a passion for travel and exploring who installed his collections of art from Asia, Africa and Oceania here. The luxurious **gardens** are magnificent, as is the **loggia** whose two sides open onto the lake. Scenes from the movies *Star Wars* and *Casino Royale* were filmed here.

Tremezzo★★

The hillsides cloaked with cypress trees, palm trees and olive trees, all the way down to the lake, make this one of the most photogenic spots on the island. The gardens and terraces of the **communal park★** lend themselves to a stroll or a picnic.

Villa Carlotta★★ – *Via Regina, 2 - ℘ 0344 40 405 - www.villacarlotta.it - Apr-mid-Oct: 9am-6:30pm; March and 2nd half of Oct: 9:30am-5pm - 10 €.*
The jewel in the crown of the villas around the lake, this captivating place cast its spell on both Stendhal and Flaubert. The land was initially owned by the Clerici family, a prominent Milanese family in the 16-18C then by the Marquis of Sommariva, a great wit, skilled financier and politician close to Napoleon, who gave the site its current appearance and the

Tremezzo by Lake Como

bulk of the artworks inside. In 1843, the villa and its collections were purchased by Prince Albert of Prussia and his wife, who bequeathed them to their daughter Carlotta (Charlotte) upon her marriage to the Duke of Saxe-Meiningen.

The villa is a shrine to 19C art, containing works by **Canova** (*Palamedes, Terpsichore Lyran,* a small plaster model with small guideline pins), **Tadolini** (a copy of Canova's *Cupid and Psyche*), **Thorvaldsen** (*Alexander the Great's Entry into Babylon*), **Hayez** (*The Last Farewell of Juliet and Romeo*).

A keen botanist, the Duke of Saxe-Meiningen helped to enrich the vast **gardens★★**, still enchanting today when the rhododendrons and azaleas bloom in spring on the terraces.

Cadenabbia★

A stupendous holiday destination in a superb location, across from Bellagio, it is linked to Tremezzo and Villa Carlotta by an avenue lined with plane trees, Via del Paradiso.

From the **St. Martin chapel** *(1 hr 30 on foot),* **view★★** of the Bellagio peninsula, the lake and the Grigne.

Menaggio★★

One of the most beautiful stations on the lake, and you can catch the ferry to Bellagio and Varenna from here. In the town center, the main road heads inland, giving way to an adorable promenade, with pretty railings and cast iron balconies offering a magnificent view of the lake. Little squares with attractive façades and fountains open onto the promenade, inviting you to stop for a drink on the terrace.

Gravedona

After **Dongo**, where Mussolini and his mistress, Clara Petacci, were captured on 27 April 1945 before being executed, you reach the final place of interest on the western shore.
In a charming natural setting on the lakefront is **Santa Maria del Tiglio★★**, a fascinating church in the Romano-Lombard style with a bell-tower in its façade, a rarity in Italy's Roman art. Inside is a wooden crucifix from the 12ᵗʰ c. and traces of frescoes.

SOUTHERN SHORE★★

The **route★** between Como and Bellagio offers some beautiful scenery *(30 km via the P 583. Take care, as the road, narrow in places, is seldom free of clutter)*.
In the enticing village of **Torno**, the San Giovanni church (14C) has a **portal★** in the Lombard Renaissance church.

80

Bellagio★★★

Long cherished for its climate and wonderful views, Bellagio is at the junction of Lakes Como and Lecco. The elegant and very touristy village first attracted Europe's jet-setting elite in the 19C, when Francesco Melzi, Duke of Lodi, had a villa built here, luring the Milanese nobility to Bellagio and pre-determining the town's vocation as a tourist hot-spot.
For exceptional **views★★** of the lake, head to the hotel Il Perlo Panorama, above the punta Spartivento, the 'point that separates the wind'.
Narrow streets lead up from the shore like staircases, lined with houses and stores selling silk goods; **Salita Serbelloni** does a roaring trade. While the **San Giacomo** church (11C), at the top, is a fine example of the Roman Lombard style, the villas of Bellagio are the city's real treasures.
Jardins de la Villa Serbelloni★★ – ☎ 031 95 15 55 - www.bellagiolakecomo.com - Mars-Oct: guided tour by appt. at 11am and 3:30pm (2:30pm in Mar and late Oct) - closed Mon and in bad weather - meet at Piazza Chiesa, 14 - 9 €. The villa, which dominates the village, was built in the 15C and 16C; the Serbelloni family expanded the park in the 18C. Now

The Madonna del Ghisallo
Cycling fans won't want to miss the small chapel of the Madonna del Ghisallo, patron saint of cyclists, at the apex of a legendary climb in the Tour of Lombardy. Beside the church, which contains a lot of memorabilia about the most famous cyclists, is a museum dedicated to cycling. Via Gino Bartalli, 4 - ☎ 031 96 58 85 - www.museodelghisallo.it - Mar-Oct 9:30am-5:30pm - 6 €.

owned by the Rockefeller Foundation in New York, it is used as a studies center. The tour of the gardens takes you to the tip of the promontory, unveiling some terrific **views** of the three-armed lake.

Gardens of Villa Melzi★★ – *1 km along the road from Como - Via Melzi d'Eril, 8 -* ℘ *33 94 57 38 38 - www.giardinidivillamelzi.it - Apr-Oct 9:30am-6:30pm - 6.50 €.* The sober neo-classical building belonged to Francesco Melzi d'Eril, Grand Chancellor of the Kingdom of Italy and a collaborator of Napoleon, who is buried in the gardens. Its ravishing **park**, on the lakefront, inspired Franz Liszt when he stayed at Bellagio in 1837. On the south side is a beautifully decorated neo-classical chapel.

RIVE ORIENTALE★

Varenna★★

53 km north-east of Bellagio and 30 km north of Lecco. Taking the ferry to Bellagio is more convenient.
This charming market town, less touristy than Bellagio, stands on a small promontory. From the jetty there is a lovely **promenade**★ overhanging the shore. From the shore, roads with stone steps take you up to the village. At the end of the promenade, **Villa Cipressi** now houses a hotel and has an enchanting **garden**.
Via IV Novembre, 18 - ℘ *0341 83 01 13 - www.varennaturismo.com - garden: Apr-Oct 8am-6:30pm - 4 €.*

Villa Monastero★ – ℘ *0341 295 450 - www.villamonastero.eu - gardens: 9:30am-7pm (10am-5pm Mar and Oct); museum: June-Sep every day except Mon 9:30am-7pm; Mar-May and Oct Fri-Sun 10am-5pm - closed Nov-Feb except Sun - gardens 5 €, museum & gardens 8 €.* A beautiful Renaissance house on the site of a former convent. Its vast **gardens**★ contain lemon trees, camellias and rhododendrons and boast some of the finest views of the lake. The villa has a **museum** with collections of paintings, tapestries and furniture from various eras.
In the heart of the village, in an alluring little square, is the medieval church **San Giorgio**, the Baroque church **Santa Maria delle Grazie** and, lastly, **San Giovanni Battista**, (frescoes from the early 14C).

Abbazia di Piona★

If you head north around the eastern shore *(13 km)*, you reach the medieval market town of **Corenno Plinio**, watched over by its castle.
Five kilometers farther on is this gracious monastery, founded in the 11C by Cluniac monks. It has a remarkable 13C Roman Lombard **cloister**★.

The western shore of Lake Garda★★★

Fondly regarded ever since Antiquity for its climate, Lake Garda is the biggest lake in Italy (370km²). Within easy reach of Trentino to the north, the Lombardy of Brescia on its western shore and the Venetia of Verona to the east, it is also the most touristy, much-loved by a German, Swiss and Austrian clientèle. It has a great variety of aspects: a low, flat coast, formed by the alluvial deposits of the southern part; sheer slopes on the western shore; the mountain range of Monte Baldo dominating the eastern shore. It has promoted mass tourism to a greater extent than the others, turning its back on the tranquility and elegance that make Lake Maggiore and Lake Como so appealing. On its western shore, the most sun-kissed and agreeable side, cedar trees and lemon trees grow, hence its nickname, the 'Lemon Riviera'.

▶**Getting there:** The lake is linked to Milan by the A4 but also by rail. ♿ *See p. 123* for info. Buses also go to Desenzano and Sirmione every hour, leaving from the bus station in Brescia - 𝒫 030 44 061 - www.trasportibrescia.it.
Map. 84. Map of Lombardy and the Lakes region (inside the cover) CD2.

SIRMIONE★★

135km east of Milan. Avoid taking a car to Sirmione in summer, when traffic makes it practically impossible to get around. The buses to Desenzano go as far as the fortress.
On the tip of a narrow, 3.5km-long peninsula, Sirmione was liked by the Romans due to its sulfurous **thermal springs**. The tradition lives on, and folks come from far and wide to take the waters, recommended for respiratory problems *(www. termedisirmione.com)*. This success was down to the area's appeal: except in the castle district, perched at the end of the tongue of land, the village, equipped for tourism above all else, now has more hotels and campsites (tourist area of Colombare) than real insights into Italian life.

Once you're past all the hotels, the small town's houses are clustered around the mighty **Rocca Scaligera★** (fortress of the Scaliger family) from the 13-15C, a wonderful ensemble with battlements with a great view of the dungeon. *Piazza Castello, 1 - 𝒫 030 91 64 68 - www.architettonicibrescia. beniculturali.it - 8:30am-7:30pm except Mon and Sun 8:30am-2pm - 4 €.*

Nearby, the church **Santa Maria Maggiore** (15C) was built with re-used ancient materials. Lovely frescoes inside.

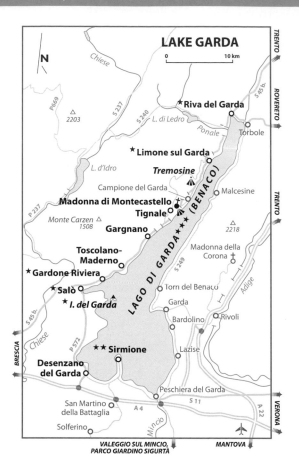

LAKE GARDA

0   10 km

TRENTO

ROVERETO

TRENTO

VERONA

BRESCIA

Chiese

P 669
△ 2203

S 237

S 240

L. di Ledro

★ Riva del Garda

Ponale
○ Torbole

★ Limone sul Garda

Tremosine

L. d'Idro

Campione del Garda

P 237

Madonna di Montecastello
Tignale

○ Malcesine

△ 2218

Monte Carzen △ 1508

Gargnano

LAGO DI GARDA ★★★ (BENACO)

Madonna della Corona †

S 249

Adige

Toscolano-
Maderno

★ **Gardone Riviera**

★ **Salò**

★ *I. del Garda*

○ Torri del Benaco
○ Garda
○ Bardolino   ○ Rivoli

S 45 b.

Chiese

P 572

★★ **Sirmione**

○ Lazise

Desenzano
del Garda

Peschiera del Garda ○

San Martino ○
della Battaglia

A 4

S 11

Mincio

A 22

Solferino ○

VALEGGIO SUL MINCIO,
PARCO GIARDINO SIGURTÀ

MANTOVA

84

At the end of the rocky promontory, at a **site★★** of great beauty, are the '**Grotte di Catullo'**, an archaeological zone where traces of an enormous Roman villa were unearthed; it is thought to have belonged to the Roman poet Catullus (circa 87-54 BC). A small **museum** tells the story of the digs. ℘ 030 91 61 57 - www.archeologica.lombardia.beniculturali.it

*- Mar-Oct: 8:30am-7:30pm, Sun
9:30am-6:30pm ; rest of the year:
8:30am-5pm (museum 7:30pm), Sun
8:30am-2pm - 6 €.*

Near here, on a promontory, the **San
Pietro in Mavino** church, built on
a former Roman temple, contains
beautiful frescoes (13-16C.).

DESENZANO DEL GARDA

9.5km west of Sirmione.

This small town is among the most
elegant on the lakefront. Attracting
mostly Italian tourists, it has a livelier,
nicer feel to it than Sirmione. Truly
buzzing in the evenings, Desenzano
has an abundance of restaurants
and nightspots. The old port, the
picturesque Malvezzi square and
the ancient neighboring town are
lovely places to meander around. The
imposing **Santa Maria Maddalena
church**, from the 16C, topped with
a dome, is home to an intense **Last
Supper**★ by Tiepolo. A promenade in
the old town leads to the **ruins of the
medieval castle** which watch over the
town. Very nice viewpoint.

To the north of this area, in Via degli
Scavi Romani, the remains of a
Roman villa dating from the 4C and
containing a beautifully preserved
polychrome mosaic were found.
*☏ 030 91 43 547 - every day except
Mon 8:30am-7pm (5pm Nov-Feb) - 2 €.*

The area around the city lends itself
to a bike-ride: you'll find maps at the
tourist office with detailed descriptions
of the routes (7-17km long) and their
stages.

SALÒ★

20km north of Desenzano.

Nicely sheltered at the end of a bay,
this peaceful market town is beautifully
situated, beside the lake. It was the
capital of the Magnifica Patria, under
Venetian rule, from the 15C through
to Napoleon's arrival in 1796. Its name
is also linked to the Italian Social
Republic, proclaimed by Mussolini in
1943, after he was overthrown, and
to Pasolini's diabolical film *Salò or
the 120 days of Sodom* (1975), a grim
image of domination inspired by Sade.
Magnolias adorn the lovely
pedestrianized **promenade**★; under
the Art nouveau façades, cafés and
restaurants open their terraces across
from the yachts. Excursions by boat to
the lake's villages leave from here.
Behind its austere brick façade, the
Duomo (15C) hides a large **polyptych**★
made of gilded wood from 1510 and
works by Moretto da Brescia and
Romanino. Near the church, the
Palazzo Fantoni (15C) has one of
Italy's most extensive libraries.
On the elegant lungolago Zanardelli,
the **Palazzo della Magnifica Patria**,
rebuilt in the early 20C, houses the
Museo civico archeologico, which has
items from the Roman era. *Lungolago
Zanardelli, 55 - ☏ 0365 20 661 - free.*

ISOLA DEL GARDA★

*☏ 328 61 26 943 - www.isoladelgarda.
com - Mar-Oct: day varies dep. on
departure port. (2 hr visit accompanied
by the owners): Barbarano, Gardone
Riviera, Salò, Manerba, Portese,
Maderno Bardolino or Garda - 25/30 €*

boat and small aperitif included - book online.
This extremely beautiful place, already inhabited in the Roman era, housed a Franciscan hermitage in the 13C which was then enlarged by St. Bernard of Sienna. In 1870, the islet came into the possession of the Duke of Ferrari, who created the imposing palace in the Venetian neo-Gothic style, then the Scipione-Cavazza family. Around the palace is a marvelous garden with local and exotic flora, maintained with great care and passion.

GARDONE RIVIERA★

4km east of Salò.
The village is spread between, near the lake, a sunny holiday resort with multiple hotels, and higher up, the village of **Gardone di Sopra**, far more picturesque.
Il Vittoriale degli Italiani★ – *Via Vittoriale, 12 - ℘ 0365 29 65 11 - www. vittoriale.it - Apr-Oct: 8:30am-7pm (Mon 10am-3:45pm for Prioria and Museo d'Annunzio Eroe); reset of the year: 9am-4pm (except Mon for Prioria and Museo d'Annunzio Eroe) - closed 24-25 Dec and 1st Jan - 16 € combined ticket for museum and gardens. In the high season, as the Vittoriale is very popular, arrive before 10am or buy tickets the day before.* Once owned by the poet **Gabriele D'Annunzio** (1863-1938). This vast estate surrounded by gardens offering a lovely view of the lake is a sort of sanctuary where people celebrate poetry, patriotism and the warlike heroism of this key figure in Italian Decadentism,

against the backdrop of fascism's tragic apogee. The neo-classical villa **La Prioria** evokes the sombre and highly-charged atmosphere in which this writer and aesthete loved to live. The **Museo d'Annunzio eroe** looks back at his activity during the First World War and the subsequent years. The park has numerous souvenirs, like the prow of the *Puglia*, aboard which D'Annunzio threw himself into the assault on Fiume, and the **Museo d'Annunzio segreto**, which shines a light on the poet's personality through his personal effects: clothes, shoes, jewelry.
Higher up, the mausoleum affords visitors a lovely **view★**.
Heller botanic garden – *Via Roma, 2 - ℘ 336 41 08 77 - www.hellergarden. com - Mar-Oct 9am-7pm - 10 €.* Situated in the lower part of the village, this charming garden is dotted with sculptures by contemporary artists and flora from five continents.

TOSCOLANO MADERNO

5km north-east of Gardone Riviera.
This market town is the perfect starting point for a foray into the **Valle delle Cartiere** (valley of the papermills), along the length of the Toscolano torrent. The **Museo della Carta** (Museum of Paper) traces the history of this traditional industry, for which the town was known from the 14-20C. *Via Valle delle Cartiere - ℘ 0365 54 60 23 - www.valledellecartiere.it - Apr-Sep: 10am-6pm; Oct: w/end. 10am-5pm - closed the rest of the year - 6 €.*

Before arriving at Gargnano, don't miss, at **Bogliaco di Gargnano**, the magnificent and imposing 18C. **Palazzo Bettoni Cazzago**.

GARGNANO

8 km north-east of Gardone Riviera.
This pleasant village is circled by lemon trees and citrons. The **San Francesco** church boasts a 15C cloister, whose Moorish-style arcades rest on capitals sculpted with oranges and lemons.
Continuing northwards, along the cliff some spectacular structures appear: these are the *limonaie*, used to help grow the lemons in accordance with a method applied since the 18C To find out more, stop off at **Limonaia del Prà de la Fam**, on the SS 45bis, jsut after a passageway. *Loc. Porto di Tignale - ℘ 334 83 97 953 - www. limonaiagarda.com - Apr-Sep: every day except Tue 10:30am-5:30pm (Sat 12:30pm-5:30pm) - 1 €.*
Retrace your steps and go through the passage to reach the market town of **Tignale**. As you walk away from the shore to get to the plateau de **Tremosine**, you'll enjoy some exceptional **views★★★** of the lake. The **sanctuary of Montecastello** looks down on the lake from a height of 800m and boasts frescoes from the school of Giotto. *℘ 0365 73 019 - Easter-Oct 9am-6pm.*

LIMONE SUL GARDA★

22km north-east of Tignale.
The name of this very picturesque village exudes the aroma of lemon: whether in greenhouses or on terraces, the tree with the golden fruit is ubiquitous here. Visit the **Limonaia del Castèl** *(Via Capitelli - ℘ 0365 95 40 08 - Apr-Oct 10am-6pm)* or the **Limonaia di Villa Boghi** *(Via IV November, 25 - ℘ 0365 95 40 08 - 9am-9pm).*

RIVA DEL GARDA★

10 km north-east of Limone.
The **old town★** will charm you with its alleyways and shops, youthful ambiance, and lively bars and pubs. Nearby, there's sport for all abilities *(info at the tourist office)*: sailing and windsurfing on the lake, climbing and mountain-biking in the mountains, trekking and canyoning, paragliding, golf, fishing, horse-riding, canoeing... Near the lake are the medieval towers of the 16C **rocca**, former residence of the prince-bishops, now home to exhibitions and the **Museo Alto Garda**, dedicated to the region's art, history and archaeology. *Piazza Cesare Battisti, 3/A - ℘ 0464 57 38 69 - www. museoaltogarda.it - mid-Mar to late Oct: 10am-6pm - closed Mon except June-Sept - 3 €.*
Parco Grotta Cascata Varone – *3km to the north - www.cascata-varone.com - Mar-Oct 9am-5pm (7pm in summer); Nov-Feb Sun 10am-5pm - 5.50 €.* In this park, visit to grottoes, walk among the waterfalls and take a trip to the botanical garden.

Addresses

Naviglio Grande
© CarmenMurillo/iStockphoto.com

🍴

Where to eat

For eating on the go and quick snacks, make sure you also check out the places listed in the *Where to drink* section (&see p. 100).

&*Use the numbered circles (e.g.* ❶*) to find the bars and restaurants on our maps. The coordinates in red (e.g. C2) refer to the fold-out map (in the inside cover).*

MILAN

DUOMO - CASTELLO SFORZESCO

Map of the area p. 17

Under 25 €

90 ⓬ **Luini Panzerotti** – *E5* - *Via Santa Radegonda, 16 -* 🚇 *Duomo -* 🕿 *02 86 46 19 17 - www.luini.it - closed Sun and Mon afternoon - 10/15 €.* Since 1949 this place has specialized in the *panzerotto*, a specialty from Puglia: pastry pockets filled with cheese and tomato, best eaten on the go right in the shadow of the Duomo.
⓭ **Pizzeria Starita** – *B3* - *Via Gherardini, 1 corner of Corso Sempione -* 🕿 *02 33 60 25 32 - www. pizzeriestarita.it - 12/17€.* 300m from the Arco della Pace, one of Naples' great *pizzaioli* has opened a branch here and it is always packed (*no reservations*). You can enjoy excellent *pizze* and other Neapolitan specialties here.
㉘ **Il Mercato del Duomo** – *E5* - *Galleria Vittorio Emanuele II -* 🚇 *Duomo -* 🕿 *02 32 06 26 828 -*

www.ilmercatodelduomo.it - 8am-10pm - 5/20 €. In a prime location on the Piazza del Duomo, 500m² dedicated to food and drink, with stalls and specific areas for different foods: pasta, cheese and cold meats, meat and fish. On the ground floor, the refurbished **Bar Motta** is one of the best-known establishments in Milan.For an aperitif, head to the 2ⁿᵈ floor where **Terrazza Aperol** offers great wine spritzers (*www.terrazzaaperol.it*); 4ᵗʰ floor wine bar *Le Bollicine del Duomo* is dedicated to tastings of the wine Franciacorta. For a gastronomic delight, head to the 3ʳᵈ floor for dinner at Spazio Milano (&see below).

25 to 50 €

㊾ **Jade Café** – *F5* - *Via Palazzo Reale, 5 -* 🚇 *Duomo -* 🕿 *02 72 09 55 35 - www.jadecafé.it - 20/40€.* A stone's throw from the Duomo, this restaurant offers Japanese, Chinese and Thai cuisine in a modern and informal setting. 10€ set menu at lunchtime.
㊽ **Spazio Milano** – *E5* - *Il Mercato del Duomo, 3ᵉ étage - Galleria Vittorio Emanuele II -* 🚇 *Duomo -* 🕿 *02 87 84 00 - www.nikoromitoformazione.com - 35/50 €.* The training school run by Michelin-starred chef Niko Romito offers this successful formula: a space dedicated to talented young chefs, concocting artful dishes at very enticing prices. Clean and contemporary setting.

50 to 75 €

① **Ristorante Giacomo Arengario** – ***E5*** *- Via Guglielmo Marconi, 1 - Duomo - 02 87 84 00 - www.giacomoarengario.com - 45/60 € - booking req'd.* This restaurant, on the 3rd floor of the Museo del Novecento (*see p. 16*), features charming 1930s-themed decor. Contemporary cuisine, panoramic views from the terrace and a very on-trend ambiance.

⑪ **Emilia e Carlo** – ***D4*** *- Via Sacchi, 8 - Duomo - 02 87 59 48 - www.emiliaecartlo.it - closed Satlunchtime and Sun - 50/70 €.* In a small building from the early 19C is this classical establishment offering contemporary, creative cuisine accompanied by an excellent wine list.

QUADRILATERO DELLA MODA AND CORSO VENEZIA

Map of the area p. 25

Under 25 €

㉔ **Nun** – ***H3*** *- Via Lazzaro Spallanzani, 36 - Porta Venezia - 02 91 63 73 15 - www.nunmilano.com - closed Mon - 8/15 €.* A tiny place that offers sandwiches made with different types of bread and fillings (kebabs, falafels, etc.), as well as vegetarian dishes. An affordable but high-quality meal, to go or to eat in.

㉞ **Chic and Go** – ***F4*** *- Via Montenapoleone, 25 - Montenapoleone - 02 78 26 48 - www.chic-and-go.com - 10am-8pm - 10/15 €.* Serves very chic, bespoke *panini*: this is the fashion district after all! You choose the type of bread and the filling: salmon, beef tartare, crab, buffalo mozzarella... Real quality that hits the spot!

Pizzeria Spontini – ***Off map beyond H2*** *- Via Spontini, 4 - Lima - 02 20 47 444 - www.pizzeriaspontini.it - 10/15 €.* Established in 1953, this ultra-simple pizzeria serves some of the best *pizze al trancio* in Milan. Only one option available (margherita) and rapid service to ensure high customer turnover.

㉝ **Panino Giusto** – ***H3*** *- Via Malpighi, 3 - Porta Venezia - 02 29 40 92 97 - www.paninogiusto.it - 10/20 €.* A chain of *paninoteche* offering tasty and original sandwiches. It's worth making a detour to see the wonderful Liberty building that houses it (*see p. 27*).

25 to 50 €

⑳ **Il Salumaio di Montenapoleone** – ***F4*** *- Via Santo Spirito, 10/Via del Gesù, 5 - Montenapoleone - 02 76 00 11 23 - www.ilsalumaiodimontenapoleone.it - closed Sun - 30/45 €.* In the enchanting setting of the Palazzo Bagatti Valsecchi (*see p. 24*), this establishment founded in 1957 serves highly acclaimed food in three sections: fine dining, mid-level restaurant, and bistro/café. The terrace is lovely in the warmer months.

㉜ **Joia Kitchen Bistrot** – ***G3*** *- Via Panfilo Castaldi, 18 - Repubblica - 02 29 52 21 24 - www.joia.it - closed Sun - 35/45 €.* The famous vegetarian restaurant run by Michelin-starred chef Pietro Leemann offers a bistro-style area where you can eat your fill

🍴

and enjoy a wonderful gastronomic experience without breaking the bank (you'll need to readjust your budget for the restaurant though!).

BRERA AND CORSO GARIBALDI

Map of the area p. 30

Under 25 €

36 **Princi** – *D3* - Largo La Foppa, 2 - 🚇 Moscova - ℘ 02 65 99 013 - *www.princi.it - 7/15 €*. A renowned bakery offering all kinds of bread, *pizze*, *focacce* and sweet and savory specialties, to be enjoyed amid the hustle and bustle of Largo La Foppa. Several locations in the city.

25 to 50 €

21 **Latteria San Marco** – *E3* - Via San Marco, 24 - 🚇 Moscova - ℘ 02 65 97 653 - *closed w/ends.* - 30/45 €. A former creamery, converted into a restaurant that serves up regional cuisine inspired by products available at the market.

😊 **35** **Pisacco** – *E2* - Via Solferino, 48 - 🚇 Moscova - ℘ 02 91 76 54 72 - *www.pisacco.it - closed Mon - 35/50 €*. This contemporary bistro, overseen by Michelin-starred chef Andrea Berton, serves food that is straightforward but never banal, in a handsome setting: the modern decor combines well with the architecture of a former depot that used to open onto the canal. 14 € set menu lunch on weekdays.

Restaurant in Brera

© anouchka/iStockphoto.com

30 **Serendib** – **D2** - *Via Pontida, 2 - ⓜ Moscova - ☏ 02 65 92 139 - www. serendib.it - closed at lunchtime - 20/40 €*. This restaurant, whose name means Sri Lanka in Old Persian, sees it as its mission to put a smile on our faces! Seductive Indian and Singhalese cuisine, true to its origins.

2 **Cittamani** – **E3** - *Piazza Mirabello, 5 - ⓜ Moscova - ☏ 02 38 24 09 35 - www.cittamani.com - closed Sun 20/40€*. Indian chef Ritu Dalmia decided to bring her delicate, gourmet cuisine to Milan and offer her guests a fusion of tradition Indian and numerous Mediterranean ingredients.

56 **Pizzeria Nazionale** – **D3** - *Via Palermo, 11 - ☏ 02 36 68 37 02 - http://lapizzerianazionale.it - 10/15 €*. Morbida o croccante? Each pizza is available in two options, either soft or crusty. There isn't a huge amount of choice, but the *pizze* are original and the ingredients are selected with care. The plants looking on from the ceiling make it feel as though you're in a little garden in the heart of the city. Very nice indeed.

50 to 75 €

6 **Pacifico** – **E3** - *Via Moscova, 29 - ⓜ Moscova - ☏ 0287 24 47 37 - www.wearepacifico.com - 40/70€*. Cosmopolitan Milan gave a warm welcome to this establishment, a taste ambassador for the flavors of Peru, blended with several Asian influences. A very wide selection of excellent *ceviches*: fish and/or seafood that is raw and marinated in lemon and flavored with several spices, such as pepper and coriander.

PINACOTECA AMBROSIANA AND OLD MILAN

Map of the area p. 33

Under 25 €

18 **Peck Italian Bar** – **E5** - *Via Cesare Cantù, 3 - ⓜ Duomo - ☏ 02 86 93 017 - www.peck.it - closed Sun and Mon lunchtimes - 20/30 €*. The young and dynamic bistro section of this legendary gastronomic establishment offers a good selection of dishes, with high-quality ingredients guaranteed.

39 **Ottimo Massimo** – **E5** - *Via Victor Hugo/Via Spadari - ⓜ Cordusio - ☏ 02 49 45 76 61 - www.ottimo massimogourmet.it - 10/20 €*. This very eco-friendly place is dedicated to fast gourmet: from morning to night you can come here for delicacies, *panini*, salads, fruit and vegetable extract and juices, served in a bright and modern setting done up in real chestnut wood.

25 to 50 €

25 **Hostaria Borromei** – **D5** - *Via Borromei, 4 - ⓜ Cordusio - ☏ 02 86 45 37 60 - www.hostariaborromei.com - closed Satlunchtime and Sun lunchtime*. This restaurant, housed in an 18C building, offers seasonal, locally-produced cuisine. The terrace is charming.

40 **Trattoria Milanese** – **D5** - *Via Santa Marta, 11 - ⓜ Cordusio - ☏ 02 86 45 19 91 - closed Sun - 35/45 €*. An old-style trattoria that serves all the classic dishes in the Milanese repertoire: *risotto allo zafferano, ossobuco, cotoletta alla milanese*.

🍴
CA' GRANDA
AND THE FORMER CANALS

Map of the area p. 38

Under 25 €
16 **Bottiglieria da Pino** – *F5* - *Via Cerva, 14 - ⓐ San Babila - ℘ 02 76 00 05 32 - closed Sun and evenings - 15/20 €.* Despite being located in a business and finance district, this classic *trattoria* has managed to retain its non-elitist nature, offering generous dishes and unbeatable prices.

25 to 50 €
Cascina Cuccagna - Un posto a Milano – *Off map beyond H7* - *Via Cuccagna, 2 - ⓐ Porta Romana - ℘ 02 54 57 785 - www.unpostoa milano.it - closed Mon - 35/50 €.* A little corner of the countryside in the city: a converted farm turned gastronomic and cultural haven. Copious lunchtime buffet for 15 €; a more thematic menu in the evening, with an emphasis on great ingredients. Also has four apartments that sleep 2/6 ppl., perfect for a rustic stay in Milan.
43 **Al Mercato** – *E6* - *Via Sant'Eufemia, 16 - ⓐ Missori - ℘ 02 87 23 71 67 - www.al-mercato.it - 30/60 €.* A dynamic burger bar, always crowded, that offers street food from all four corners of the globe or, for the most discerning customers, a gourmet restaurant with great meat dishes. Set menu on weekday lunchtimes for 10 €.

50 to 75 €
3 **Giacomo Bistrot** – *H5* - *Via Sottocorno, 6 - ℘ 02 76 02 26 53 - www.giacomobistrot.com - 50/80 €.* There's a plush atmosphere at this refined bistro, serving international cuisine non-stop, 24 hrs a day. Velvet seating, leather-bound tomes on the shelves and subdued lighting.

PORTA TICINESE, NAVIGLI
AND SOLARI DISTRICT

Map of the area p. 44

Under 25 €
47 **Panino Lab alla Ferramenta** – *A6* - *Via Montevideo, 8 - ⓐ Porta Genova - ℘ 02 22 22 00 34 - www.paninolab.it - closed Sun eve and Mon eve - 10/15 €.* A former ironmongery dating from 1927 was turned into a first-rate *paninoteca*. Delicious sandwiches and great care taken over the ingredients.
48 **Il Kiosko** – *D7* - *Piazza 24 Maggio - ⓐ Porta Genova - ℘ 02 89 40 22 24 - www.ilkiosko24maggio.it - 10am-10pm - closed Sun afternoon - 10/15 €.* On the square that opens onto the Darsena, this fishmonger's offers fish fritters, fish burgers and *arancini* to have in. Delicious.
54 **Gino Sorbillo - Olio a Crudo** – *B6* - *Via Montevideo, 4 - ⓐ Porta Genova - ℘ 02 58 10 47 89 - 10/15 €.* Setting the benchmark for Neapolitan pizza in Milan, with three restaurants (the others are at *11 Largo Corsia dei Servi,* and *19 Via Agnello, Duomo district).* As its name suggests, they add the oil at the end of the cooking process here, for a lighter and more flavorsome pizza.

94

25 to 50 €

5 Trattoria Madonnina – *D7* - *Via Gentilino, 6 - ⌂ Porta Genova - ℘ 02 89 40 90 89 - closed Sun and Mon-Tues eve - 25/40 €.* This small Milanese restaurant from the early 20C has changed little: the furniture, posters, and photos are all from that era. Simple and flavorsome cuisine. Outside, there are some stone tables beneath a gazebo.

44 Drogheria Milanese – *C6* - *Via Conca del Naviglio, 7 - ⌂ Sant'Ambrogio - ℘ 02 58 11 48 43 - www.drogheriamilanese.it - 25/35 €.* A warm and pleasant place that offers tasting menus or a more traditional menu. Enjoy simple but mouthwatering specialties like Cantabrian anchovies, *zola* cheese with champagne or black kale soup. Young and relaxed atmosphere.

☺ 45 Al Fresco – *A7* - *Via Savona, 50 - ⌂ Porta Genova - ℘ 02 49 53 36 30 - www.alfrescomilano.it - closed Mon - 35/60 €.* A former industrial depot that has been transformed into a flower-filled garden, where the restaurant's dining spaces are laid out. The specialties on the menu celebrate Italian tradition. Try the *spaghetti di Gragnano* with a sauce of bottarga, almonds, anchovies and Sorrento cedar, or crispy octopus with a sauche of beans in paprika, marinated courgettes and lemon confit.

46 Cantina della Vetra – *D6* - *Via Pio IV, 3 - ℘ 02 89 40 38 43 - www.cantinadellavetra.it - closed Mon lunchtime - 30/50 €.* In a magnificent location behind the San Lorenzo basilica and across from the park, this place with its rustic vibe offers a cuisine rooted in the traditions of the Bel Paese (the beautiful country).

10 Rebelot – *B7* - *Ripa di Porta Ticinese 55 - ⌂ Porta Genova - ℘ 02 84 19 47 20 - www.rebelotnavigli.com - closed lunchtimes except Sun - 25/40 €.* In the bohemian district of the Navigli, a bistro that offers taster menus and cocktails in a youthful and relaxed setting.

50 to 75 €

4 Langosteria – *B6* - *Via Savona, 10 - ⌂ Porta Genova - ℘ 02 58 11 16 49 - http://langosteria.com - closed lunchtimes and Sun - 50/80 €.* For lovers of seafood, this restaurant will be a real revelation: carpaccios, oysters and seafood form the basis of its cuisine, not forgetting of course the fish, all of which is wild. An excellent wine cellar and a glamorous setting complete the picture.

8 Esco Bistrò Mediterraneo – *A7* - *Via Tortona 26 - ⌂ Porta Genova - ℘ 02 83 58 144 - www.escobistrot mediterraneo.it - closed Sat lunchtime and Sun - 25/50 €.* A modern concept restaurant, welcoming and informal; at first it feels as if you're sitting at a guest table in an architecture studio. The chef's delicious food deftly combines high-quality products, technique and innovation. 14€ set menu at lunchtime during the week.

Over 75 €

29 Enrico Bartolini al Mudec – *A7* - *Via Tortona, 56 - ⌂ Porta Genova - ℘ 02 84 29 37 01 - www.enrico bartolini.net - closed Mon lunchtime and Sun - 90 € and up.* The ultra-contemporary setting of the Mudec museum hosts one of the best restaurants in the city. The cooking of Enrico Bartolini, a real star of Italian gastronomy, is balanced, innovative and sought-after. On the ground floor of the same building, the **Mudec Bistrot** serves simpler and more affordable fare. ☎ 02 84 29 37 06 - www.enricobartolini.net - closed evenings except Thurs and Sat - 15/40€.

SANT'AMBROGIO AND CORSO MAGENTA

Map of the area p. 48

Under 25 €

37 **De Sanctis** – **D5** - Corso Magenta, 87 - 🚇 Cadorna or Cairoli - ☎ 02 72 09 51 24 - www.paninidesantis.it - 10/15 €. More than 200 combinations of bread and fillings can be ordered at this tiny joint, which has been filling Milanese stomachs with its *panini* since 1982.

26 **Pizzeria Da Biagio** – **B4** - Via Vincenzo Monti, 28 - 🚇 Cadorna - ☎ 02 49 87 166 - closed Sat - 15/20 €. A traditional establishment that is very well-known in the area, offering excellent *pizze* in a 1950s setting.

27 **Stelline Caffè** – **B5** - Corso Magenta, 61 - 🚇 Cadorna - ☎ 02 97 68 70 38 - www.stellinecaffe.it - 9am-6pm - closed w/ends unless there's an exhibition on - 10/20 €. Wander into the Palazzo delle Stelline to discover the cloisters, order a sandwich or salad with coffee and sit down to enjoy them in the delightful garden, a verdant hidden gem in the heart of the city.

50 to 75 €

49 **La Brisa** – **D5** - Via Brisa, 15 - 🚇 Cairoli ou Castello - ☎ 02 86 45 05 21 - www.ristorantelabrisa.it - closed Sun lunchtime and Sat - 45/60 €. Across from a Roman-era archaeological site, a modern trattoria that serves locally-produced cuisine; in summer, the veranda opens out onto the garden for outdoor eating.

17 **Zero Milano** – **A5** - Corso Magenta, 87 - 🚇 Conciliazione - ☎ 02 45 47 47 331 - www.zeromagenta.com - closed lunchtimes and Mon - 40/60€. The classics of Japanese cuisine are all present and correct here, but the soul of this restaurant lies in its 'zero' dishes, the result of a blend of western cuisine and partial flame-grilled cooking. Booking advisable at the sushi bar.

PORTA NUOVA AND NORTHERN DISTRICTS

Pull-out map.

Under 25 €

42 **Pizzeria Berberè** – **E1** - Via Sebenico, 21 - 🚇 Isola - ☎ 02 36 70 78 20 - www.berberepizza.it - closed lunchtimes except w/ends. People come here to try a pizza with a variety of toppings or enjoy some *cicchetti*, delicious appetizers. The quality is first-rate. This is a popular eatery, so expect a line.

25 to 50 €

50 **Il Bue e la Patata** – **E1** - Via Luigi Porro Lambertenghi, 24 - 🚇 Isola - ☎ 02 39 82 05 24 - www.ilbuela patata.com - 25/40 €. On the menu:

primarily (but not exclusively) meat and potatoes served in a variety of ways. A relaxed restaurant in the heart of the vibrant and popular Isola district. Also serves *pizze*. 13€ lunchtime menu on weekdays.

51 **Osteria del Treno** – *G2* - *Via San Gregorio, 46 - Repubblica - 02 67 00 479 - www.osteriadeltreno.it - closed at lunchtime on w/ends - 25/35 €.* A typical *osteria* offering a menu centered around Milanese tradition, based on carefully chosen ingredients. The ravishing Sala Liberty was once the lounge of the train-drivers' union's offices, hence the restaurant's name.

50 to 75 €

9 **Bon Wei** – *A1* - *Via Castelvetro, 16/18 - Gerusalemme - 02 34 13 08 - www.bon-wei.it - closed Mon lunchtime - 45/60 €.* Next to Milan's Chinatown, a refined establishment offering creative Cantonese cuisine. One of the best Chinese restaurants in Milan.

Iyo – *Off map beyond A1* - *Via Piero della Francesca, 74 - Gerusalemme - 02 45 47 68 98 - www.iyo.it -closed Mon and Tues lunchtime - booking req'd - 40/80 €.* This gourmet restaurant offers the favorites of Japanese cuisine (sushi, sashimi, teppanyaki) but also creative and 'fusion' dishes, with the focus shifting back westwards for the desserts, which you select from a mouthwatering dessert tray. Superb food in a refined setting.

52 **Ratanà** – *F1* - *Via De Castilla, 28 - Isola ou Gioia - 02 87 12 88 55 - www.ratana.it - 45/60 €.* A dynamic

establishment housed in a Liberty building that was once a cinema and then a railway depot. Great attention is paid to the ingredients and the local traditions. Charming terrace opening out onto the park. 19 € lunch menu on weekdays and aperitifs from 6:30pm.

OFF THE MAP

25 to 50 €

Shambala – *Off map, beyond G8* - *Via Ripamonti, 337 - 02 55 20 194 - www.shambalamilano.it - closed Sun eve - 40/55 €.* Around an enchanting oriental garden that transports you far away from Milan, Shambala, 'the place of happiness', serves expertly-crafted Vietnamese and Thai cuisine, with lovely background music. Great selection of cocktails. Serves Sunday brunch.

BERGAMO

LOWER TOWN

25 to 50 €

M1.lle – *Not on map* - *Viale Papa Giovanni XXIII, 18 - 035 42 20 121 - www.millestoriesapori.it - 30/45 €.* A modern and eclectic establishment, part-bistro, part-wine bar and part-restaurant, serving lovingly crafted food in an original setting.

Ol Giopì e la Margì – *Not on map* - *Via Borgo Palazzo, 27 - 035 24 23 66 - www.giopimargi.eu - closed Sun evening and Mon - 20/45 €.* The name refers to the puppets of Bergamo and the temperament of the Bergamese, while the cuisine and the waiters in costume pay homage to the town and the region. Cheese and dessert trolleys to round off your meal.

Sarmassa – _Not on map_ - _Vicolo Bancalegno, 1H -_ ☎ _035 21 92 57 - www.sarmassa.com - closed Sun - 35/50._ Meat, cold cuts and cheeses can be enjoyed beneath the vaults and arches dating from the 13C in this restaurant, which has an undeniable cachet.

UPPER TOWN

City map p. 60

25 to 50 €

㉗ Vineria Cozzi – _A1_ - _Via Bartolomeo Colleoni, 22 -_ ☎ _035 23 88 36 - www.vineriacozzi.it - set lunch menu 10/17 € (wkdays) - 25/40 €._ A delicious and welcoming place with local cuisine that is never run-of-the-mill. You can also order picnic hampers here.

㉙ La Colombina – _A1_ - _Via Borgo Canale, 12 -_ ☎ _035 26 14 02 - www.trattorialacolombina.it - closed Mon - 20/30 €._ A simple and friendly restaurant, on the outside of the city walls. The food is inspired by the seasons and by tradition.

Baretto di San Vigilio – _Off map, beyond A1_ - _Via Castello, 1 -San Vigilio -_ ☎ _035 25 31 91 - www.baretto. it - 40/60 €._ This restaurant at the San Vigilio cable-car stop serves lovely food and delicious pastries. Summer terrace with superb views of the city.

LAKE MAGGIORE

25 to 50 €

Lido Angera – _Hotel Lido Angera - Viale Libertà, 11 -_ **Angera** _(1 km to the north) -_ ☎ _0331 93 02 32 - www. hotellido.it - closed Mon lunchtime - 35/50 €._ Modern dishes that bring fresh, locally-sourced foods to the fore, through delicious and original recipes. Don't miss sushi from lake fish.

Lo Scalo – _Piazza Vittorio Emanuele, 32 –_ **Cannobio** - ☎ _0323 71 480 - www.loscalo.com - closed Tues lunchtime and Mon - 40/60 €._ A great spot that is really worth stopping for! Eat in either the rustic dining room or on the lakeside terrace, and enjoy a fresh take on traditional cuisine.

Il Vicoletto – _Vicolo del Poncivo, 3 -_ **Stresa** - ☎ _0323 93 21 02 - www. ristorantevicoletto.com - closed Thurs and Jan-Feb - 30/45 €._ Tucked away in a side-street, this place has modern decor and a kitchen that is bang on trend. Small terrace in summer.

Osteria del Castello – _Piazza Castello, 9 -_ **Verbania-Intra** - ☎ _0323 51 65 79 - www.osteriacastello.com - closed Sun - 25/45 €._ A remarkable place, located right in the town center. Extensive range of wines and Italian cuisine, best sampled in summer beneath the pergola.

Il Burchiello – _Corso Zanitello 3 -_ **Verbania-Pallanza** - ☎ _0323 50 45 03 - closed Tues. - 25/45 €._ A lovely dining space and a beautiful terrace with views of the lake: a pleasant setting in which to try great Italian cuisine in a hospitable atmosphere.

LAKE ORTA

Under 25 €

Enoteca Al Boeucc – *Via Bersani, 28 -* **Orta San Giulio** - *ℰ 339 58 40 039 - alboeuc.beepworld.it - closed Tues and Jan-Feb. - 25/35 €.* In a little street in a pretty village, a typical, and typically welcoming, establishment where you can enjoy a nice glass of wine accompanied by plates of cured meats and cheeses.

LAKE COMO

Under 25 €

Aperitivo et al – *Salita Serbelloni, 34 -* **Bellagio** - *ℰ 031 95 15 23 - www. aperitivobellagio.com - 15/25 €.* At the end of lively Salita Serbelloni, this small wine bar offers an extensive selection of light dishes: sandwiches, cured meats, salads and pastries.

Gastronomia Castiglioni – *Via Cesare Cantù, 9 -* **Como** - *ℰ 031 26 33 88 - www.castiglionistore.com - 11am-2:30pm - closed Sun - 17/25 €.* An historic grocery store (founded in 1958) containing a restaurant and wine cellar *(Via Rovelli, 17).*

25 to 50 €

Terrazza Barchetta – *Salita Antonio Mella, 13 -* **Bellagio** - *ℰ 031 95 13 89 - www.ristorantebarchetta.com - closed Tues except in summer and Nov.- Easter - 30/50 €.* Inventive cuisine, with a range of specialties from the lake and from Lombard tradition. Beside it, **Ristoro** serves more straightforward dishes and *pizze*, to have in or take out.

Crotto del Sergente – *Via Crotto del Sergente, 13 -* **Como***, Loc. Lora - ℰ 031*
28 39 11 - www.crottodelsergente.it - *closed Satlunchtime - 30/40 €.* Close to the Silk museum, this former *crotto* (a natural cavity used as a wine cellar) is now used solely for the tasting of locally-sourced cuisine.

Osteria il Pozzo – *Piazza Garibaldi -* **Menaggio** - *ℰ 0344 32 333 - closed Wed. and Nov-Feb - 30/40 €.* Pleasant trattoria serving delicious dishes in generous portions, inspired by Frioul. Good price-quality ratio.

LAKE GARDA

25 to 50 €

Agriturismo Il Bagnolo – *Loc. Bagnolo - Serniga, 1 km north- west of* **Gardone Riviera** - *ℰ 0365 20 290 - www.ilbagnolo.it - closed lunchtimes except Satand Jan-Feb - booking advisable - 25/30 €.* An outdoor restaurant in an enchanting area, this 'agritourism' spot serves delicious dishes based on farm-grown products.

Kapuziner am See – *Via Dante, 39 -* **Riva del Garda** - *ℰ 0464 55 92 31 - www.kapuzinerriva.it - fermé fév. - 25/40 €.* On the ground floor of the Hotel Vittoria, this much-loved Bavarian restaurant marries Bavarian specialties with Italian ones; it serves German beers and Italian wines.

Antica Contrada – *Via Colombare 23 -* **Sirmione** - *ℰ 030 99 04 369 - www. ristoranteanticacontrada.it - closed Tues lunchtime and Mon - 35/50 €.* 2km from the city center, a restaurant for those with classic taste, whose cuisine pays homage to seafood specialties. Intimate terrace, very nice indeed in the summer months.

Where to drink

After a long day's sightseeing or shopping, there's nothing quite like a good *aperitivo* (a *happy hour* for the Milanese). For a fixed price (approx. 8-15 € depending on the bar), between 6pm and 9pm you can have a drink and help yourself to an ample buffet of cured meats, raw vegetables and other appetizers. It's an ideal formula which might just take the place of dinner some nights.

Use the numbered circles to locate the bars and restaurants on the maps e.g. ❶). The coordinates in red (e.g. C2) refer to the fold-out map (in the inside cover).

MILAN

DUOMO - CASTELLO SFORZESCO

Map of the area p. 17

❷ **Camparino in Galleria** – *E5* - Galleria Vittorio Emanuele II - Duomo - ℘ 02 86 46 44 35 - www.camparino.it - 7:15am-8:40pm - closed Mon. The Liberty interior of this café, opened in 1867 at the same time as the Galleria, was designed in 1915. This Milanese institution was reproduced by the futurist Boccioni in his work *Riot in the gallery* (housed at the Pinacoteca di Brera, *see p. 29*).

❹❼ **Pasticceria Marchesi** – *E5* - Galleria Vittorio Emanuele II (1st floor) - Duomo - ℘ 02 94 18 17 10 - www.pasticceriamarchesi.com - 7:30am-9pm. One of the great names in the Milanese pastry scene is opening its new outlet in the city's *salotto*. In a very elegant space with a panoramic view of the gallery, you can enjoy the sweet treats that are the house's specialty.

❶❼ **Duomo 21 Terrace** – *E5* - Via Silvio Pellico, 2 - Duomo - ℘ 02 45 39 76 54 - www.duomo21.it - 11am-9pm. With its magnificent view of the cathedral and the Museo del Novecento, the terrace of this lounge bar is the perfect spot for an aperitif (approx. 15 €) in fine weather.

❸❹ **Sky Terrace Hotel Milano Scala** – *E4* - Via dell'Orso, 7 - Duomo - ℘ 02 87 09 61 - www.skyterracemilanoscala.it - 6pm-11pm, Sun 11am-2:30pm - booking req'd. A 360° panorama of the entire city: that's what the menu offers at this elegant café which presents itself as a real *greenhouse* (complete with winter version). Excellent aperitifs (*15 €*) accompanied by an original and quality range of *finger food*.

❸ **Café Trussardi** – *E4* - Piazza della Scala, 5 - Duomo - ℘ 02 80 68 82 95 - www.trussardiallascala.com - 7:30am-11pm, Sat 12pm-11pm - closed Sun. Inside the modern Palazzo Trussardi, next to the prestigious Teatro alla Scala. Refined and very busy at aperitif time.

❹ **Giacomo Caffè** – *E5* - Piazza del Duomo, 12 - Duomo - ℘ 02 89 09 66 98 - www.giacomocaffe.com - 7:30am-7:30pm (Thurs and Sat 10:30pm). Under the arcades of the Palazzo Reale, visit this inviting literary café where you can leaf through a beautiful tome while taking a break upstairs.

5 Triennale Design Café – *C3* - *Viale Emilio Alemagna, 6 - Parco Sempione - Cadorna - 02 23 05 82 45 - www.triennale.org/visita/ caffe-e-ristorante - 10:30am-8:30pm - closed Mon* Housed inside the Triennale Design Museum, this very well-lit and pleasant café is a terrific place for an aperitif or for Sunday brunch *(booking required)*. In summer, you can sit in the lovely garden adorned with sculptures.

26 Galleria Meravigli Bistrot – *D5* - *Via Meravigli, 3 - Cordusio - 02 39 83 12 31 - www.galleriameravigli.com - 7am-6pm, Sun 12pm-4pm.* In a pretty gallery dating from 1928 that has been restored, this elegant and well-lit café is open from breakfast through to aperitif time.

QUADRILATERO DELLA MODA AND CORSO VENEZIA

Map of the area p. 25

6 Pasticceria Cova – *F4* - *Via Montenapoleone, 8 - San Babila - 02 76 00 55 99 - www.pasticceria cova.it - 7:45am-8:30pm, Sun 9am-9pm.* An historic little place, founded in 1817, that's perfect for a coffee break. Across the street, there's hot competition from **Marchesi** (**12** *Via Montenapoleone, 9*).

27 Emporio Armani Caffè – *E4* - *Via Croce Rossa, 2 - Montenapoleone - 02 72 31 86 80 - armanirestaurants. com - 8am-9pm.* The café inside the Armani megastore serves breakfast,

lunch and aperitifs. Luxury without ostentation and fine Italian cuisine.

15 H Club – *H3* - *Hotel Sheraton Diana Majestic - Viale Piave, 42 - Porta Venezia - 02 20 58 20 81 - www.hclub-diana.it.* Sit back in one of the armchairs placed under the trees in the garden of this gorgeous hotel built in 1907. It's a delightful spot and the *aperitivo* comes in a generous serving, as does the weekend brunch.

Bar Basso – *Off map beyond H2* - *Via Plinio, 39 - Lima - 02 29 40 05 80 - www.barbasso.com - closed Mar.* This is the bar where the Negroni *sbagliato* (or 'Negroni gone wrong') was invented. The original ingredients are red vermouth, Campari and gin. For the 'wrong' version, sparkling wine is used instead of gin. Not to be missed

50 Lavazza Flagship Store – *E4* - *Piazza San Fedele, 2 - Duomo - 7:30am-8:30pm (w/end 8:30am).* In the historic heart of the city, the big Turin-based firm has opened an ultra-modern space in which you can dive into the multisensory world of coffee.

28 Caruso Fuori Restaurant Bar – *E4* - *Piazzetta Croce Rossa - Montenapoleone - 02 72 31 41 - www.grandhoteletdemilan.it - 10am-10pm - closed Sun afternoon.* There's wonderful decor akin to that of a Parisian bistro at this café at the Grand Hotel de Milan. The terrace is the perfect setting for something sweet or for an aperitif.

32 Illy Caffè – *F4* - *Via Montenapoleone, 19 - Montenapoleone - 02 83 54 93 86 - 8am-11pm -* In the center of Quadrilatero della Moda, the major coffee company offers an elegant space with a pleasant courtyard for the summer. Great for brand-name breakfasts, something sweet or a light meal.

25 Bicerin – *G3* - *Via Panfilo Castaldi, 24* - *Porta Venezia* - *02 84 25 84 10* - *www.bicerinmilano.com* - *3pm-12am, Sun 5pm-12am*. You'll feel as if you're in a private house in this welcoming and well-stocked wine-bar run with passionate dedication by three young friends.

BRERA AND CORSO GARIBALDI

Map of the area p. 30

8 Bulgari – *E4* - *Hotel Bulgari - Via privata Fratelli Gabba, 7/b* - *Montenapoleone* - *02 80 58 051* - *www.bulgarihotels.com*. This hotel offers delicious cocktails (*22 € approx.*) in a very zen-like ambiance or ravishing garden, a real oasis of calm. *For those looking for a hyper-trendy space.*

9 Bookshop e Caffetteria degli Atellani – *E3* - *Via Moscova, 28* - *Moscova* - *02 36 53 59 59* - *www. atellani.it* - *12pm-6pm* - *closed w/ends*. Located next to the Santa Teresa media library, this modern glass cube, reminiscent of a tropical greenhouse, is ideal for a coffee or aperitif.

11 Fioraio Bianchi Caffè – *E3* - *Via Montebello, 7* - *Moscova* - *02 29 01 43 90* - *www.fioraiobianchicaffe.it* - *8am-midnight* - *closed Sun* A very romantic place in which to sip an aperitif or have a coffee among the flowers - for the café just happens to be a florist's, as well.

13 RivaReno – *D4* - *Via Mercato, 20* - *Lanza* - *02 89 09 66 31* - *www. rivareno.com* - *1pm-11pm, Sat 1pm-12am*. This ice cream parlor offers tasty, creative flavors. Among the ones that stand out are pine nut flavor and white chocolate and puffed rice.

29 Farage Cioccolato – *E4* - *Via Brera, 5* - *Lanza* - *02 78 62 36 98* - *www.faragecioccolato.it* - *8am-7pm (Sun 12pm-7pm)*. A scrumptious patisserie and chocolaterie with elegant decor, ideal for a first-rate snack before (or after) visiting the pinacoteca di Brera.

30 Bottiglieria Moscatelli – *D3* - *Corso Garibaldi, 93* - *Moscova* - *02 65 54 602* - *2:30pm-10pm - closed Sun* Benefiting from the vibrancy of Corso Garibaldi, this wine-bar, opened in 1859, is the right spot for a *happy hour* for 8 €. Characterful setting and a pleasant terrace outside.

31 Le Rosse – *D3* - *Corso Garibaldi, 70* - *Moscova* - *02 92 87 04 16* - *www.lerosse.it* - *12:30pm-3pm, 6:30pm-12am - closed Sun* The name means 'the reds' and it refers to the Berkel slicers used for the hams and cured meats, highlights at this quirky *salumi-bar*. Cheese platters and hot dishes also available.

40 Chinese Box – *D2* - *Corso Garibaldi, 104* - *Moscova* - *02 65 54 564* - *www.chinesebox.bar* - *8pm-2am, Sun 6pm-2am*. A very popular place that serves cocktails and aperitifs at unbeatable prices. Modern and dynamic ambiance on the lively Largo La Foppa.

PINACOTECA AMBROSIANA AND OLD MILAN

Map of the area p. 33

14 **Pasticceria Panarello** – ***E5*** - *Via Speronari, 3 -* Duomo *- ℰ 02 86 46 22 64 - www.panarello.com - 8am-7pm.* A place so typically Milanese (founded in 1930) that you forget it's in fact a Genoese patisserie. Several outlets, with the most recent addition at 52, Via della Moscova.

CA' GRANDA AND FORMER CANALS

Map of the area p. 38

16 **Taveggia** – ***G5*** - *Via Visconti di Modrone, 2 -* San Babila *- ℰ 02 76 28 08 56 - www.taveggia.it - 7am-9pm (Sun8am-8pm).* One of the city's historic cafés, founded in 1909 and frequented by the stars of La Scala, where you can try unforgettable specialties like the *budino di riso,* a tart with rice flour.

33 **Pasticceria Giovanni Galli** – ***E6*** - *Corso di Porta Romana, 2 - ℰ 02 86 45 31 12 - www.giovannigalli.com - 8:30am-1pm, 2pm-8pm, Sun 9am-1:30pm.* Founded in 1911, this patisserie specializes in producing marrons glacés, chocolates, marzipan and delicious Boeri - cherries dipped in cognac then covered with brown sugar and chocolate.

PORTA TICINESE, NAVIGLI AND SOLARI DISTRICT

Map of the area p. 44

18 **La Hora Feliz** – ***D6*** - *Via San Vito, 5 (derrière San Lorenzo) -* Missori *-*
ℰ 02 83 76 587 - 5pm-2am. A little corner of Cuba in Milan, with a great selection of cocktails and a buffet that's piled extremely high!

19 **El Brellin Caffè** – ***C7*** - *Vicolo Lavandai, corner of Alzaia Naviglio Grande, 14 -* Porta Genova *- ℰ 02 58 10 13 51 - www.brellin.com - 12:30pm-3pm, 6:30pm-1am.* In the charming Vicolo Lavandai, a pleasant spot to have a drink while looking at the artworks on display, or enjoying some good music.

35 **Sacrestia Farmacia Alcolica** – ***C8*** - *Via Conchetta, 20 - ℰ 02 89 45 48 13 - www.sacrestia.com - 12pm-2am, w/end 6pm-2am - closed Mon evening.* The eclectic and original decor at this cocktail-bar and restaurant tells the tale of its history: in the early 20th century there was a brothel here, then in the 1950s, a pharmacy.

7 **Liquidambar** – ***B7*** - *Hotel Magna Pars Suites - Via Forcella, 6 -* Porta Genova *- ℰ 02 83 78 111 - www.magnapars-suitesmilano.it - 10am-1am - closed Sun* A former perfume factory, transformed by its owners into a designer hotel. Inside, there's a gourmet restaurant (**Da Noi In**), a hidden garden, the LabSolue perfume studio and this lounge bar, perfect for an aperitif. Don't miss the quirky 'aperitivo olfattivo', celebrating the site's history in the perfume business.

SANT'AMBROGIO AND CORSO MAGENTA

Map of the area p. 48

21 **Shockolat** – *Via Boccaccio, 9 -* ***C4*** *-* Cadorna *- ℰ 02 48 10 05 97 - www.*

10 Corso Como Café

chocolatmilano.it. Very close to Santa Maria delle Grazie. There's a fantastic range of chocolaty flavors at this on-trend ice cream and pastry store.

22 **Pasticceria Marchesi** – **D5** - *Via S. Maria alla Porta, 11/a - Cairoli - 02 86 27 70 - www.pasticceriamarchesi.it - 7:30am-8pm, Sun 8:30am-1pm - closed Mon* Founded in 1824, this spot abounds with charming retro details and treats that will drive you crazy, like the delicious chocolates and fruit confits.

36 **BoccascenaCafé** – **C4-5** - *Teatro Litta - Corso Magenta, 24 - Cadorna - 392 92 43 823 - www.teatrolitta.it/boccascenacafe. html - 10am-9pm, Mon 10am-4pm,*

Sat 6pm-9pm - closed Sun The café at the charming Teatro Litta is a lovely space, both outside in the courtyard with its clock-tower, or in a room dominated by a huge fountain that was once a drinking trough for horses.

PORTA NUOVA AND NORTHERN DISTRICTS

Pull-out map

51 **Il Massimo del Gelato** – **A1** - *Via Castelvetro, 18 - 02 34 94 943 - http://ilmassimodelgelato.it - closed Mon* This ice-cream parlor attracts locals from all four corners of the city. A plethora of original flavors and some winning, chocolaty tones.

24 Cantine Isola – *C2* - *Via Paolo Sarpi, 30 - ⊚ Garibaldi - ℘ 02 33 15 249 - closed Mon* In the heart of the Chinese district, a very popular *enoteca* with an extensive wine-list. The crowd here often spills out onto the sidewalk.

10 10 Corso Como Café – *E2* - *Corso Como, 10 - ⊚ Garibaldi - ℘ 02 29 01 35 81 - www.10corsocomo.com - 10:30am-1am.* Located inside Carla Sozzani's *concept store*, this café has a minimalist and refined style, reflecting the elegance of Milan. The terrace is a haven for birds, with several species putting in an appearance.

1 Terrazza Gallia – *G1* - *Excelsior Hotel Gallia - Piazza Duca d'Aosta, 9 - ⊚ Centrale - ℘ 02 67 85 35 14 - www.terrazzagallia.com - 12pm-midnight.* On the 7th floor of the luxurious Hotel Gallia, this terrace provides a panoramic perspective, so you can sip at a cocktail while admiring the bustle of the city.

37 Deus Café – *E1* - *Via Thaon di Revel, 3 - ⊚ Isola - ℘ 02 83 43 92 30 - deuscustoms.com/cafes/milan.* Via Thaon di Revel has become a sort of motorcycle-themed street. Why? Well, Deus ex Machina, the legendary Australian manufacturer of motorcycles, surfboards, skateboards and bikes, opened a café here that embodies the Deus philosophy. Lunch, aperitifs, dinner or brunch can be had here, but always book ahead!.

38 Mint Garden Café – *G2* - *Via Felice Casati, 12 - ⊚ Repubblica - ℘ 02 83 41 78 06 - www.mintgardencafe.it.* A flower store converted into an adorable café-cum-bistro, which blends the beauty of the flowers with culinary delights. An ideal spot for anything from breakfast to aperitifs.

39 Pavé – *G2* - *Via Felice Casati, 27 - ⊚ Repubblica - ℘ 02 94 39 22 59 - www.pavemilano.com - 8am-8pm (8:30am-7pm on w/ends) - closed Mon* A young and dynamic café-cum-patisserie whose culinary lab creates irresistible sugary specialties, such as miniature tarts.

41 Gelato Giusto – *H2* - *Via San Gregorio, 17 - ⊚ Repubblica - ℘ 02 29 51 02 84 - www.gelatogiusto.it - 12pm-11pm - closed Mon* High-quality ice cream, made by a master who trained at the great culinary schools of London and Paris. The result is fabulous: there's no point trying to describe it, you'll just have to try it!

BERGAMO

UPPER TOWN

City map p. 60

43 Caffè della Funicolare – *B1* - *Via Porta Dipinta, 1 - ℘ 035 21 00 91 - caffedellafunicolare.it - closed Tues.* Situated, as its name suggests, at the upper cable-car station, this café has neo-Gothic decor and a terrace that overlooks the lower town.

44 Pasticceria Cavour – *A1* - *Via Gombito, 7/A - ℘ 035 24 34 18 - 7:30am-8:30pm - closed Wed.* This historic café still has its decor from the 19th c., when it was a meeting place for artists passing through Bergamo. Its specialty: the Cavour tart, made of meringue, nuts and chocolate.

🛍 *Shopping*

Milan is one of the shopping capitals of the world. The shopping streets with the highest footfall, where you'll find lots of international chains, are: Corso Vittorio Emanuele II, Via Dante, Via Torino, Corso Buenos Aires, Corso Vercelli and Corso Genova. The boutiques of the young designers tend to be found in the Isola and Porta Ticinese districts.

Ⓒ Use the numbered circles to locate the stores on the maps (e.g. ❶). The coordinates in red (e.g. C2) refer to the fold-out map (in the inside cover).

MILAN
DUOMO - CASTELLO SFORZESCO

Map of the area p. 17
Fashion
❶ **La Rinascente** – *E5* - *Via Santa Radegonda, 3* - 🚇 *Duomo* - ℘ *02 88 521* - *www.rinascente.it* - *9:30am-10pm.* Milan's most famous and chic department store contains all the major labels in ready-to-wear fashion. The 7th floor is dedicated to food and restaurants of every variety. Italian and international cuisine can be found here, right across from the spires of the cathedral.
❷ **Borsalino** – *E5* - *Galleria Vittorio Emanuele II, 92* - 🚇 *Duomo* - ℘ *02 89 01 54 36* - *www.borsalino.com* - *10am-7pm* - *closed Sun in the summer.* The showroom of the famous millinery offers a vast range of men's and ladies' hats.

㉛ **Prada** – *E5* - *Galleria Vittorio Emanuele II, 63* - 🚇 *Duomo* - ℘ *02 87 69 79* - *www.prada.com.* A brand new space for the historic brand in Milanese fashion. Having had a presence in the gallery since its creation in 1913, the fashion house now shares it with the offices of its Foundation.
㉜ **Versace** – *E5* - *Galleria Vittorio Emanuele II, 33* - 🚇 *Duomo* - ℘ *02 89 01 14 79* - *www.versace.com.* A magnificent new store in Milan's *salotto* (living room) for this brand, an iconic one for the city and for fashion.

Leather goods
❹ **Furla** – *E5* - *Piazza Duomo, 31* - 🚇 *Duomo* - ℘ *02 89 09 67 94* - *www.furla.com* - *10am-9pm.* Superior quality, sober lines, elegance, functionality and innovation are the hallmarks of the collections by Furla, a firm established in 1927 in Bologna.

Bookstores
❺ **Feltrinelli** – *E5* - *Piazza Duomo/ Via Ugo Foscolo 1/3* - 🚇 *Duomo* - ℘ *02 86 99 68 97* - *www.lafeltrinelli.it* - *9:30am-9:30pm (Sun 10am-8pm).* In the basement of Caffè Motta, this space offers visitors a bookstore section and a space for music. Other outlets: Via Manzoni 12, Stazione Centrale, Stazione Garibaldi, Piazza Piemonte 2, Corso Buenos Aires 33, Corso 22 Marzo 4, Piazza Gae Aulenti and the ground floor of the brand new Fondazione Feltrinelli (*Viale Pasubio, 5*).

QUADRILATERO DELLA MODA AND CORSO VENEZIA

Map of the area p. 25

Fashion and jewelry

3 Excelsior Milano – *F5* - *Galleria del Corso, 4 -* ⊚ *Duomo* - ☏ *02 76 30 73 01 – www.excelsiormilano.com - 10am-8:30pm.* The former Excelsior cinema, redesigned by Jean Nouvel, houses a large luxury store offering accessories, fashion-wear and design items, across seven floors.

7 Max Mara – *F5* - *Piazza Liberty 4/Corso Vittorio Emanuele II -* ⊚ *San Babila* - ☏ *02 76 00 88 49 - www.maxmara.com - 10am-8pm.* A brand with a relaxed and dynamic style.

13 Apple Store – *F5* - *Piazza Liberty, 1 -* ⊚ *San Babila - www.apple.com* Apple's new flagship store is concealed below ground, behind a 10m glass fountain that you have to go through in order to reach the retail location. Well worth seeing.

8 DMagazine – *F4* - *Via Bigli, 4 -* ⊚ *Montenapoleone* - ☏ *02 36 64 38 88 - www.dmagazine.it - 10am-7:30pm.* In the heartlands of Milanese fashion, this store offers knock-offs of the major labels. Other retail outlets at Via Manzoni 44 and Via Forcella 13 (Solari district).

9 Aspesi – *E4* - *Via Montenapoleone 13 -* ⊚ *Montenapoleone* - ☏ *02 76 02 24 78 - www.aspesi.com - closed Sun* A very attractive store dedicated to the famous brand, with its elegant and relaxed style.

10 Gallo – *F4* - *Via Manzoni, 16 -* ⊚ *Montenapoleone* - ☏ *02 78 36 02 - www.gallospa.eu - 10am-7:30pm.* This is the perfect place to stock up on colorful and on-point cotton socks.

11 Pellini – *F4* - *Via Manzoni, 20 -* ⊚ *Montenapoleone* - ☏ *02 76 00 80 84 - www.pellini.it - 9:30am-7:30pm - closed Mon am and Sun* For three generations, the Pellini family has been making gorgeous jewelry, characterized by the use of hard stones, fine stones and resins.

46 Pirelli Corso Venezia – *F4* - *Corso Venezia, 1 -* ⊚ *San Babila* - ☏ *02 64 42 42 42 - www.pirellidesign.com - 12:30am-7:30pm - closed Sun* This spectacular flagship store celebrates both the industrial and technological side and the fashion aspect of Pirelli, which, with the brands Pirelli PO and Pirelli Design, also produces clothes and shoes.

Design and the home

12 Alessi Flagship Store – *E4* - *Via Manzoni, 14/16 -* ⊚ *Montenapoleone* - ☏ *02 79 57 26 - www.alessi.com - closed Sun* The store of this famous producer of household goods is an elegant space measuring 170 m^2 divided into four sections, including the **Museo**, where the firm's best-known items are displayed.

14 ē DePadova – *G4* - *Via Santa Cecilia, 7 -* ⊚ *San Babila* - ☏ *02 77 72 01 - www.depadova.it - 10am-7pm - closed Sun* An historic store in Milanese design where, for almost 60 years, the best in Italian accessories and furniture has been housed (Castiglioni, Cerri, Magistretti...).

15 Frette – *F4* - *Via della Spiga, 31 -* ⊚ *Montenapoleone* - ☏ *02 78 39 50 - www.frette.com - 10am-7pm (Sun 11am-6pm).* A firm founded in 1860, offering a wide range of very classy household linen.

Bookstores

6 Hoepli - *E4* - *Via Hoepli, 5 -* San Babila - *02 86 48 71 - www.hoepli.it - 10am-7:30pm - closed Sun* A historic Milanese bookstore, founded in 1870 by Ulrico Hoepli and run by the same family ever since. Remarkable selection of books on design and architecture.

BRERA AND CORSO GARIBALDI

Map of the area p. 30

Fashion and perfume

17 Cavalli & Nastri - *E4* - *Via Brera 2 -* Montenapoleone - *02 72 00 04 49 - www.cavallienastri.com - 10:30am-7:30pm, Sun 12pm-7:30pm.* A ravishing boutique in the heart of the Brera district, which sells vintage dresses, shoes, bags and jewelry.

36 Traifiori - *E2* - *Via Solferino, 31 -* Moscova - *02 29 00 25 63 - www.traifiori.com - 10:30am-7pm - closed Sun-Mon* This luminous and charm-filled spot is the perfect setting for the elegant and refined knitwear of Marillina Lunardon. Knitted fabrics, scarves and accessories beneath origami flowers falling like raindrops.

37 Profumo - *E4* - *Via Brera, 6 -* Lanza - *02 72 02 33 34 - www.profumomilano.com - 10am-7pm - closed Sun* A sumptuous perfume store selling high-end artisan perfumes.

18 Alfonso Garlando - *D4* - *Via Madonnina, 1 -* Lanza - *02 87 46 65 - www.alfonsogarlando.it - 10am-7:30pm, Mon 12:30-7:30pm.* The best place for artisan shoes for 30 years now, with an endless range of models and colors.

Stationery stores

35 Fabriano Boutique - *D4* - *Via Ponte Vetero, 17 -* Lanza - *02 76 31 87 54 - www.fabrianoboutique.eu - 10am-7:30pm, Sun 11am-1pm, 2pm-7pm.* An historic name in Italian stationery welcomes you at this beautiful boutique, in a part of town filled with artists and students from the Fine Arts academy.

Gastronomy and wine

23 Eataly Milano Smeraldo - *E2* - *Piazza XXV Aprile, 10 -* Garibaldi - *02 49 49 73 01 - www.eataly.net - 8:30am-12am.* The former Smeraldo theatre, converted in 2014, is now home to a 500 m² space dedicated to bio Italian food, spread over three floors with retail outlets and themed restaurants. On the first floor, the hall *Il Palco dello Smeraldo* hosts shows and concerts.

34 Enoteca Cotti - *E2* - *Via Solferino, 42 -* Moscova - *02 29 00 10 96 - www.enotecacotti.it - 9am-1pm, 3pm-8pm - closed Sun and Mon* This historic store, founded in 1952, sells more than 1000 wines, but also oil, vinegar, sweet products and chocolate. A real Ali Baba's cave!

Design and the home

45 Cargo High Tech - *E2* - *Piazza XXV Aprile, 12 –* Garibaldi - *02 62 41 101 - www.cargomilano.it - 10:30am-7:30pm, Mon 1:30pm-7:30pm, Mon 1:30pm-7:30pm.* The workshops of a former ink factory that supplied ink to the *Corriere della*

Sera now house 2000 m² dedicated to design, decoration and fashion.

PINACOTECA AMBROSIANA AND OLD MILAN

Map of the area p. 33

Fashion

21 **Wait and see** – *D5* - *Via Santa Marta, 14* - Missori - ☎ *02 72 08 01 95* - *www.waitandsee.it* - *10:30am-7:30pm, Mon 3:30pm-7:30pm - closed Sun* The space created by designer Uberta Zambeletti sells ladies' fashion and objects from all over the world.

Jewelry

38 **DDM - Daniela De Marchi** – *D5* - *Via dei Piatti, 9* - Missori - ☎ *02 86 99 50 40* - *www.danielademarchi.it* - *10:30am-2:30pm, 3:30pm-7:30pm - closed Sun-Mon* Hidden in the heart of Milan, this workshop makes magnificent silver, bronze and brass jewels, embellished with enamels, quartz, amethysts or cornelian. Its trademark is the *dropage* technique, where the surface of the jewels is decorated with little balls.

CA' GRANDA AND THE FORMER CANALS

Map of the area p. 38

Fashion

33 **Brian & Barry** – *F5* - *Via Durini, 28* - San Babila - ☎ *02 76 00 55 82* - *www.brianebarry.it* - *10am-8pm (stores)*. A 12-story building dating from the 1950s and designed by architect Giovanni Muzio (1893-1982)

houses this department store dedicated to fashion, beauty, accessories and design. There are also eateries here and, on the top floor, there's **Terrazza 12**, a café with a magnificent panoramic terrace: the right place for an *aperitivo con vista* (*www.terrazza12.it* - *12pm-1am*).

Design and the home

22 **Danese** – *F6* - *Piazza San Nazario in Brolo, 15* - Missori - ☎ *02 58 30 41 50* - *www.danesemilano.com* - *11:00am-1:30pm, 2:30pm-7pm, Mon 3pm-7pm - closed Sun* A place that sets the standard for fans of design, with contemporary objects and historic pieces by the great names in Italian design.

Bookstore

39 **Open** – *G7* - *Viale Monte Nero, 6* - Porta Romana - ☎ *02 58 30 41 50* - *www.openmilano.com* - *9am-9pm, Sat10am-7pm - closed Sun* 'More than books': this place lives up to its motto. Open is at once bookstore, café, design store, space for work and relaxation, and digital and hard-copy newspaper archive. Has a young, dynamic and very pleasant vibe.

Pâtisserie

40 **Ernst Knam** – *H6* - *Via Anfossi, 10* - Porta Romana - ☎ *02 55 19 44 48* - *www.eknam.com* - *10am-1pm, 4pm-8pm, Mon 4pm-8pm, Sun 10am-1pm.* The German Ernst Knam, an honorary Milanese, is the 'king of chocolate'. His creations are such works of art that you almost don't want to eat them, so as not to spoil their beauty. Their sublime taste forces the issue though!

PORTA TICINESE, NAVIGLI AND SOLARI DISTRICT

Map of the area p. 44

Fashion

24 **Frip** – *D6* - *Corso di Porta Ticinese, 16 - ☎ 02 83 21 360 - www. frip.it - 11am-2pm,3pm-7:30pm, Mon 3pm-7:30pm - closed Sun* For 23 years, this has been a go-to place for ultra-hip *urbanwear*, with niche items from Scandinavia and the UK. A section of the store is dedicated to CDs and vinyl records.

26 **Wok Store** – *D7* - *Viale Col di Lana, 5 - ☎ 02 89 82 97 00 - www. wok-store.com - 12pm-7:45pm, Sat3pm-7:45pm - closed Sun* A *concept store* selling items (fashion and accessories) by young artists and designers.

41 **Wag** – *C6* - *Via De Amicis, 28 - ☎ Sant'Ambrogio - ☎ 02 80 53 063 - 9am-7:30pm, Mon 3:15pm-7:30pm.* A cult store for fans of *street culture* and hip-hop, established in 1990. You'll find T-shirts and baseball caps created by famous *street artists* and other must-have accessories.

Markets

27 **Mercatone dell'Antiquariato** – *BC7* - *Naviglio Grande, from Viale Gorizia to the bridge on Via Valenza - ☎ Porta Genova - ☎ 02 94 09 971 - www.navigliogrande.mi.it.* On the last Sunday of each month, this antiques market makes for a very pleasant stroll of almost 2km along the Naviglio.

SANT'AMBROGIO AND CORSO MAGENTA

Map of the area p. 48

Fashion and perfume

28 **Marinella Cravatte** – *D5* - *Via Santa Maria alla Porta. 5 - ☎ Cordusio - ☎ 02 86 46 70 36 - www. marinellanapoli.it - 10am-7pm - closed Sun* The Milanese branch of the famous tie manufacturer founded in Naples in 1914. Other retail location: Via Manzoni, 23.

29 **Pérfume by Calé** – *D5* - *Corso Magenta, 22 - ☎ Cairoli - ☎ 02 80 50 94 49 - www.cale.it - 10am-7:30pm, Mon 12:30pm-7:30pm - closed Sun* In a pure and minimalist space, a perfume store specializing in high-end artisan products.

Design and the home

30 **Galleria Rossana Orlandi** – *B5* - *Via Matteo Bandello, 16 - ☎ Conciliazione - ☎ 02 46 74 471 - www.rossanaorlandi.com - 10:30am -7:30pm - closed Sun* A former manufacturing site transformed by Rossana Orlandi into a hip, eclectic space where you can find fashion, design, artisan goods and an art gallery. Charming shaded garden.

CDs and vinyl

42 **Buscemi Dischi** – *C5* - *Corso Magenta, 31/Via Terraggio - ☎ Cadorna - ☎ 02 80 41 03 - www. buscemidischi.it - 10am-1pm, 3pm-7:30pm, Mon 3pm-7:30pm - closed Sun* THE place to go to buy music in the city, specializing in vinyl and rare editions. Unmissable place for music-lovers.

111

🛍

Stationery stores

㊸ Ercolessi – *C5* - *Corso Magenta, 25 - ⓜ Cadorna - ☏ 02 86 45 24 44 - www.ercolessi.gpa.it - 10am-2pm, 3pm-7pm, Mon 3pm-7pm - closed Sun* Since 1921, this boutique has been a Mecca for anyone who loves pens and pen accessories. All the brands are here, as are many limited editions.

Gastronomy

㊹ Drogheria Soana – *D5* - *Corso Magenta, 1 - ⓜ Cairoli - ☏ 02 86 45 27 25 - 8:30am-1pm, 3:30pm-7:30pm, Mon 1:30pm-7:30pm - closed Sun Drogherie* (grocery stores) are few and far between in central Milan, but this one, founded by the Soana family in 1947, has retained the atmosphere of bygone years. It sells tea in bulk, pasta, spices, natural essences.

PORTA NUOVA AND NORTHERN DISTRICTS

Pull-out map

Fashion and jewelry

⑯ 10 Corso Como – *E2* - *Corso Como, 10 - ⓜ Garibaldi - ☏ 02 29 00 26 74 - www.10corso como.com - 10:30am-7:30pm (Wed. and Thurs 9pm).* The gallery owner Carla Sozzani has created an avant-garde venue with a New York vibe: it houses an art gallery, bookstore, restaurant, café, B&B and a store offering all manner of trendy items (clothing, accessories, perfume, etc.). A shrine to Milanese hipster-ism!

⑳ Monica Castiglioni – *E1* - *Via Pastrengo, 4 - ⓜ Garibaldi - ☏ 02 87 23 79 79 - www.monicacastiglioni.com - Thurs-Sat 11am-8pm.* The daughter of designer Achille Castiglioni designs wonderful jewels, displayed at the MoMa in New York and the Victoria & Albert Museum in London, England.

BERGAMO
Map p. 60

Gastronomy

㊽ Angelo Mangili – *A1* - *Via Gombito, 8 - Ville Haute - ☏ 035 24 87 74 - 8:30am-1:30pm, 3:30pm-8pm, Mon 8:30am-1:30pm.* As soon as you enter, you'll want to buy everything: cured meat, wines, and conserves.

LAKE COMO

Fashion

Picci – *Via Vittorio Emanuele II, 54 - **Como** - ☏ 031 26 13 69 - 9am-7:30pm, Mon 3pm-7:30pm, Sun 10:30am-1:30pm, 2:30pm-7pm.* For three generations, the Picci family have been creating silk items: ties, shawls, and fabrics.

Nightlife

Milan is one of the most vibrant artistic and cultural scenes in the world. Every year, the stars of classical music, rock, jazz and the theater come to the city. You can find out what's on at www.vivimilano. it on in *Vivimilano*, the Wednesday supplement in the *Corriere della Sera*. The trendiest areas for the Milanese *movida* (nightlife) are Brera (*see p. 28*), the Navigli *(see p. 44)* and Corso Como *(see p. 51)*. Corso Sempione, near the Arco della Pace, is for the really young crowd.

♪ Use the numbered circles to find the locations on our maps (e.g. ①). The coordinates in red (e.g. C2) refer to the fold-out map (in the inside cover).

© Mats Silvan/age fotostock

Teatro alla Scala

MILAN

DUOMO - CASTELLO SFORZESCO

Map of the area p. 17

Classical music

② **Teatro alla Scala** – *E4* - *Piazza Scala* - Ⓜ *Duomo* - ℘ *02 86 07 75 - www.teatroallascala.org - booking mandatory (by tel. or online) - info at the Duomo subway station.* A rite of passage for all lovers of opera, but you'll need to book a long time in advance, and buying the pricier tickets doesn't always guarantee a good view. The season opens on the feast day of St. Ambrose, 7 December.

Theater

③ **Piccolo Teatro** – *D3-4* - ℘ *02 42 41 18 89 - www.piccoloteatro. org.* Founded in 1947 by two of the greats of the Italian stage – Paolo Grassi and Giorgio Strehler – the 'Piccolo' has three stages and offers a varied selection of classic and experimental productions: **Teatro Strehler** - *Largo Greppi, 1 -* Ⓜ *Lanza;* **Teatro Grassi** - *Via Rovello, 2 -* Ⓜ *Cordusio;* **Teatro Studio** - *Via Rivoli, 6 -* Ⓜ *Lanza.*

QUADRILATERO DELLA MODA AND CORSO VENEZIA

Map of the area p. 25

14 **Armani Privé** – ***EF4*** - *Via Gastone Pisoni, 1 - Montenapoleone - 02 62 31 26 55 - armanipriveclub.com - from 11:30pm - closed Sun-Tues and Thurs - booking req'd.* Located under the restaurant Nobu, Giorgio Armani's very exclusive club is another shrine to the city's party-all-night spirit.

BRERA AND CORSO GARIBALDI

Map of the area p. 30

Cinema

4 **Anteo Palazzo del Cinema** – ***E2*** - *Via Milazzo, 9 - Moscova - https://anteo.spaziocinema.18tickets.it* - The new Anteo Palace of Cinema has 11 theaters showing films in the original English version, and feature films. In the Sala Nobel Eataly you can enjoy a meal while watching a movie.

CA' GRANDA AND THE FORMER CANALS

Map of the area p. 38

Classical music

7 **Conservatorio di Musica Giuseppe Verdi** – ***G5*** - *Via Conservatorio, 12 - San Babila - 02 76 21 10.* Chamber music and orchestral music featuring some of the world's greatest soloists. *To see what's on go to www.seratemusicali.it and www.soconcerti.it.*

PORTA TICINESE, NAVIGLI AND THE SOLARI DISTRICT

Map of the area p. 44

Classical music

8 **Auditorium di Milano** – ***C8*** - *Largo Gustav Malher - 02 83 38 94 01 - www.laverdi.org.* Classical music, jazz and musicals in a magnificent concert hall with wooden furnishings.

Cinema

Cinema Mexico – ***Off map beyond A7*** - *Via Savona, 57 - Porta Genova - 02 48 95 18 02 - www.cinemamexico.it.* English-language films shown Thursdays, and since 1980, *The Rocky Horror Picture Show* Fridays, with interactive theater after the screening.

Bars and clubs

17 **Le Biciclette** – ***C6*** - *Via Torti, 2 - 02 58 10 43 25 - www.lebiciclette.com - 6pm-2am, Sun brunch 12pm-4pm.* Amid eclectic decor that pays homage to the bicycle (once central to the life of this re-purposed industrial space), this venue serves aperitifs and food and also helps promote young musicians.

Peugeut is Bobino Club – ***Off map beyond A8*** - *Alzaia Naviglio Grande, 116 - 02 36 55 90 70 - http://bobino.it - Thurs-Sun 7pm-3am -booking advisable.* A New York-style lounge, which offers themed nights as well.

For more info see the website.

12 **Santeria Social Club** – ***E8*** - *Viale Toscana, 31 - 02 22 19 93 81 - http://www.santeria.milano.it - 11am-2am.* A converted former industrial space

now houses this restaurant, bar and theater, where you can see concerts, movies, shows and cultural events.

PORTA NUOVA AND NORTHERN DISTRICTS

Pull-out map

Bars and clubs

😊 **5** **Blue Note** – *E1* - *Via Pietro Borsieri, 37 - ⊛ Isola - ℘ 02 69 01 68 88 - www.bluenotemilano.com - closed Mon* Little brother to the famous Blue Note club in New York, Milan's most famous jazz club hosts renowned performers in an eclectic program that includes jazz, soul, world music and blues.

Alcatraz – *Off map beyond D1* - *Via Valtellina, 25 - ⊛ Maciacchini - ℘ 02 69 01 63 52 - www.alcatrazmilano.com.* Located in a reconverted industrial space, this is Milan's biggest nightclub; it is also used for fashion shows, concerts and parties. Great music.

Club Haus 80s – *Off map beyond D1* - *Via Valtellina, 21 - ⊛ Maciacchini - ℘ 389 465 22 47 - www.clubhaus80s. com.* At a former industrial wasteland, this is the ideal destination for anyone seeking a little '80s nostalgia.

18 **Il Gattopardo Café** – *A1* - *Via Piero della Francesca, 47 - ℘ 02 34 53 76 99 - www.ilgattopardocafe.com - 6pm-5am - closed Mon and in summer.* Since 2001 this former church has hosted a popular disco and bar. Aperitifs available from 6pm.

Garage Italia – *Off map beyond A1* - *Piazzale Accursio, 86 - ℘ 02 33 43 18 57 - http://garageitaliacustoms.*

it/concept - 9am-2am. The Agip gas station designed by architect Mario Bacciocchi in 1952 has been home, since 2017, to this space designed by Lapo Elkann and dedicated – as family traditions dictate, he is the grandson of Gianni Agnelli – to the automobile. The restaurant section, divided into a high-class restaurant and relaxed bar-cum-bistro, is run by chef Carlo Cracco.

OTHER DISTRICTS

La Salumeria della musica – *Off map beyond G8* - *Via Antonio Pasinetti, 4 - ℘ 02 56 80 73 50 - www.lasalumeriadellamusica.com - closed Sun* In a disused factory, a place to listen to great music while tucking into some cured meat.

LAKE MAGGIORE

Grand Hôtel des Îles Borromées – *Corso Umberto I, 67 - **Stresa** - ℘ 0323 93 89 38 - www.borromees.com - 6pm-12am.* If you can't spend a night at this hotel whose illustrious guests have included Ernest Hemingway, Rockefeller and Sacha Guitry, at least enjoy the café's beautiful terrace!

LAKE COMO

Birrificio di Como – *Via Paoli, 3 - **Como** - ℘ 031 50 50 50 - www.ilbirrificio.it - 12pm-2pm, 7:30pm-12:30am.* Located outside the city center, towards the motorway, this large brasserie and restaurant serves artisan beer.

115

Where to stay

⟳ Use the numbered circles to locate the stores on the maps (e.g. ①). The coordinates in red (e.g. C2) refer to the fold-out map (in the inside cover).

MILAN

Accommodation in Milan is very expensive and you may have to pay up to four times the usual price depending on when you visit; during major conferences and shows, it is almost impossible to find a double room for less than 200 €/night. A good solution if you want to reduce your accommodation costs, particularly for stays of 4-5 days, is to rent an apartment. Check the websites: www.airbnb.com, www.interhome.com, www.homelidays.com or www.locappart.com.

Youth hostels – The following establishments offer dorm beds, but also rooms for 2/4 or 6 people, with a private bathroom, at affordable prices (20 to 80 €/night per person).

⑪ **Ostello Burigozzo 11** – *D7* - *Via Burigozzo, 11* - ⓜ *Missori* - ☎ *02 84 17 99 69* - *http://ostello-burigozzo-11.hotels-milan.info/it* - *23 rooms 30/200 € -* 🍽 *3 €*. Great location, close to the city center and the Navigli.

⑫ **Ostello Bello** - *D5* - *Via Medici, 4* - ⓜ *Missori* - ☎ *02 36 58 27 20* - *www.ostellobello.com* - *10 rooms 70/250 €* 🍽. 500m from Piazza Duomo, with breakfast buffet

116

included in the price. The aperitifs and the brunch here are very popular. This chain also has another location: **Ostello Bello Grande** - *Via Roberto Lepetit, 33 (Stazione Centrale district)* - ☎ *02 02 67 05 921*.

⑳ **New Generation Hostel Urban Brera** – *F2* – *Via Renzo Bertoni, 3* - ⓜ *Turati* - ☎ *02 65 56 02 01* - *www.newgenerationhostel.it* - *26 rooms 30/200 € -* 🍽 *3 €*. A modern hostel in a great location; part of the New Generation Hostel network (*has other hostels in the city too, see online for details*).

DUOMO - CASTELLO SFORZESCO

Pull-out map

90 to 150 €

② **Hotel Nuovo** – *F5* - *Piazza Beccaria, 6* - ⓜ *Duomo* - ☎ *02 86 46 05 42* - *www.hotelnuovomilan.com* - *15 rooms - 100/180 €* 🍽. In a quiet little square 200m from the cathedral, this hotel offers unpretentious but well-equipped rooms, with air-con, flat-screen TVs and wifi.

150 to 250 €

④ **Hotel Genius Downtown** – *D4* - *Via Porlezza, 4* - ⓜ *Cairoli* - ☎ *02 72 09 46 44* - *www.geniushoteldowntown.com* - *38 rooms - 150/190 €* 🍽. In a quiet street just off Via Dante, this cozy hotel has modern, well-equipped rooms.

Over 200 €

5 **Antica Locanda dei Mercanti** –
D4 - Via San Tomaso, 6 - ⓜ Cordusio -
☏ 02 80 54 080 - www.locanda.it -
12 rooms - 200 € and up ☕. For a
charming stay in the heart of the city,
here's an elegantly decked-out little
hotel. Most of the bright and spacious
rooms come with a terrace.

CA'GRANDA
AND THE FORMER CANALS

Pull-out map

150 to 250 €

15 **Hotel Zurigo** – **E6** - Corso Italia,
11/a - ⓜ Missori - ☏ 02 72 02 22 60 -
www.hotelzurigo.com - 42 rooms -
120/200 € ☕. This old building with
its classical decor contains some
modern and very comfortable rooms.
Pleasant little garden and bicycles
available for guests.

PINACOTECA AMBROSIANA
AND OLD MILAN

Pull-out map

150 to 250 €

3 **Gran Duca di York** – **D5** - Via
Moneta, 1 - ⓜ Duomo - ☏ 02 87 48 63 -
www.ducadiyork.com - 33 rooms -
180/260 € ☕. Contained in an 18th c.
palace, the Gran Duca di York is a
peaceful hotel with bright colors and
a classical elegance.

© Antica Locanda dei Mercanti

117

Antica Locanda dei Mercanti

PORTA TICINESE, NAVIGLI
AND SOLARI DISTRICT

Pull-out map

90 to 150 €

19 **Cocoon** – **B7** - Via Voghera, 7 -
ⓜ Porta Genova - ☏ 02 83 22 769 -
www.cocoonbb.com - 3 rooms -
95/115 € ☕. In the middle of the Solari
district, a B&B with snug, well-tended
rooms that also has a pleasant garden.

150 to 250 €

8 **La DimORA Residence** – **D6** - Via
Vetere, 1/a - ⓜ Sant'Ambrogio - ☏ 02
58 11 11 22 - www.oradimora.com -
6 apartments. - 160/200 € ☕. Housed
in an historic building, this residence

offers apartments with all creature comforts; fully-equipped kitchenette, Wi-Fi and small garden or balcony.

16 Art Hotel Navigli – *B7* - *Via Fumagalli, 4 - ⌂ Porta Genova - ✆ 02 89 438 - www.arthotelnavigli.com - 103 rooms - 150/200 € ⌷.* Located in an ultra-hip area, this hotel has modern art on the walls (Arnaldo Pomodor, Dalì, Man Ray) and very well-equipped rooms furnished with contemporary style. Abundant American-style breakfast buffet and lovely garden for relaxation.

⌂ 10 Maison Borella – *C7* - *Alzaia Naviglio Grande, 8 - ⌂ Porta Genova - ✆ 02 58 10 91 14 - www.hotelmaison borella.com - 30 rooms - 160/250 € ⌷.* In the irresistible setting of an old Milanese house with inner courtyard, this charming hotel offers modern comfort and sober, elegant rooms. Good breakfast buffet, with homemade cakes and fresh fruit.

21 Hotel Milano Navigli – *D7* - *Piazza Sant' Eustorgio, 2 - ✆ 02 36 55 37 51 - www.hotelmilanonavigli.it - 22 rooms - 150/250 € ⌷.* In the pleasant and very lively Porta Ticinese district, a new arrival, with a contemporary vibe and a good eye for design. The rooms are minimalist and have all mod-cons.

Over 200 €

6 Nhow Milano – *A7* - *Via Tortona, 35 - ⌂ Porta Genova - ✆ 02 48 98 861 - www.nhow-hotels.com - 246 rooms - 200 € and up.* The hotel reflects the atmosphere here in the design district. The color scheme, green ceilings, clever lighting and creative decor make it more than just a place to stay.

118

PORTA NUOVA AND NORTHERN DISTRICTS

Pull-out map

90 to 150 €

9 Hotel Charly – *H2* - *Via Settala, 76 - ⌂ Caiazzo or Lima - ✆ 02 20 47 190 - www.hotelcharly.com - 20 rooms - 90/180 € ⌷.* A very pleasant and quiet spot, inside two small Liberty villas. The bright, cozy rooms look out over a quiet street or the pleasant garden.

Hotel San Francisco – ***Off map beyond H2*** - *Viale Lombardia, 55 - ⌂ Loreto - ✆ 02 23 60 302 - www.hotel-sanfrancisco.it - 30 rooms - 80/200 € ⌷.* Located in the university district, this small hotel offers an excellent price-quality ratio. Ask for a room overlooking the pretty internal garden, where breakfast is served in summer.

18 LaFavia Four Rooms – *D1* - *Via Carlo Farini, 4 - ⌂ Monumentale - ✆ 347 78 42 212 - www.lafavia4rooms. com - 4 rooms - 100/125 € ⌷.* A presentable and welcoming B&B where the decor reveals the owners' passion for travel. The names of the rooms speak for themselves: Barceloneta, LaIndia, Oaxaca and LaPalmera. Lovely flowery terrace.

BERGAMO
City map p. 60

150 to 250 €

18 Piazza Vecchia – *Via Colleoni, 3/5 - ✆ 035 25 31 79 - www.hotelpiazzavecchia.it - 13 rooms 140/240 €.* This small, family-run hotel, in a 14C, townhouse, offers elegant rooms with a wonderful view of the city.

LAKE MAGGIORE

90 to 150 €

Hotel Rigoli – *Via Piave, 48 -* **Baveno** *- ℘ 0323 92 47 56 - www. hotelrigoli.com -* 🅿 *- closed Nov.-Easter - 31 rooms - 120/150 € - ✖.* Spacious rooms with modern decor and light colors. Holiday atmosphere, especially on the terrace-garden beside the lake, where there is a splendid view of the Borromeo Islands.

Hotel Cannero – *Piazza Umberto I, 2 -* **Cannero Riviera** *- ℘ 0323 78 80 46 - www.hotelcannero.com -* 🅿 *- closed Nov-Feb. - 71 rooms - 130/170 € ☕ -* ✖. Directly overlooking the lake, an elegant establishment with cozy rooms, swimming pool, relaxation room, tennis court and restaurant serving international cuisine.

LAKE ORTA

90 to 150 €

Hotel La Contrada dei Monti – *Via dei Monti, 10 -* **Orta San Giulio** *- ℘ 0322 90 51 14 - www. lacontradadeimonti.it - closed Oct.-Mar- 17 rooms 110/160 € ☕.* A little jewel of light and harmony inside an 18th c., century palace, lovingly restored. Every last detail at this hotel is extraordinary; an enchanting place to stay for romantic types.

LAKE COMO

90 to 150 €

Il Perlo Panorama – *Via Valassina, 180, 2.5 km from the center of* **Bellagio**, *on the Como road - ℘ 031 95 02 29 - www.ilperlo.com -* 🅿 *- 18 rooms 80/140 € ☕ -* ✖. A magnificent view awaits you at this hotel, on the strip between the two branches of the lake. Impeccable rooms, with balcony, or charming fully-furnished studios.

150 to 250 €

Agriturismo Tre Terre – *Località Coslia,* **Pianello del Lario** *- ℘ 03 44 86 366 - www.treterre.it -* 🅿 🏊 *- closed Nov-Mar - 8 rooms 135/210 € ☕ -* ✖. Agritourism that is really worth it! After climbing a steep hill (it's worth it for the panoramic view), you'll find rooms with all mod-cons, decorated tastefully, a private garden and a heated pool. Breakfast buffet centered around home-made foods. Honey and jam available to buy.

LAKE GARDA

90 to 150 €

Hotel Pace – *Piazza Porto Valentino, 5 -* **Sirmione** *- ℘ 030 99 05 877 - www.pacesirmione.it - 22 rooms - 130/150 €.* This early 20th c. residence, which boasts some illustrious former guests including James Joyce and Ezra Pound, is in the historic center, across from the lake. Well-furnished rooms with a comfortable lounge area. Private garden with deckchairs and a jetty over the lake.

119

Planning Your Trip

Know before you go

Basic information

Festivals and events

BikeMi station, Piazza del Duomo
© tostphoto/iStockphoto.com

Know before you go

FORMALITIES

Documents – For residents of the EU and Switzerland, an ID card is sufficient. For everyone else, a valid passport with at least six months validity is required.

Customs – No duty-free allowance. The regulations on imported goods (alcohol, cigarettes, etc.) are the same throughout the European Union. For more details, se ec.europa. eu/taxation_customs/individuals/travelling/entering-eu_en.

GETTING TO THE LAKES REGION

Lake Maggiore

By car – From Milan, access via the A8 to the Vergiate interchange (55km). For the Lombard shore, take the SS 629; for the Piedmontese shore, take the A8 until you reach the exit for Lago Maggiore, then the SS 33.

By bus – Departing from Milan (Malpensa Airport), the Alibus stops at all the local towns on the Piedmontese shore as far as Intra, www.safduemila.com - booking required.

By train – For the Piedmontese shore: regular line between Milano Centrale or Milano Garibaldi and Verbania via Arona and Stresa (journey time 1h15m); the station in Verbania is 8km west of the city, towards Stresa.

For the Lombard shore, trains leave from Milan Cadorna for Laveno-Mombello Nord (journey time 1h45 m).

Lake Orta

By car – Instead of rejoining Orta San Giulio via the main highways (SS 229), take the scenic route through the mountains, leaving from Stresa, which goes via Gignese and Armeno (approx. 40 km). For the classic itinerary, follow the freeway A26 (take the Arese exit), then head towards Borgomanero and Gozzano (90 km).

By bus – Saf Duemila bus departing from Stresa (Lake Maggiore) – www.safduemila.com.

Lake Como

By car – From Milan, take highways A8 then A9. Travel 50 km until you reach Como.

By bus – From the bus station (Piazza Matteotti, in the center of Como), there are frequent connections with ASF to all the local towns around the lake and Bergamo. ☏ 031247249 - www.sptlinea.it.

By train – Main station in Como: Como Nord Lago for trains stopping at the local towns from Milan (1 hr). Ferrovie Nord – www.ferrovienord.it.

Lake Garda

By car – From Milan, you can get to the lake via freeway A4 (expect heavy traffic towards Milan in the morning and towards Venice in the afternoon). Exit the freeway at Desenzano del Garda (125km east of Milan).

By train – Stations on the southern shore: Desenzano and Peschiera, each approx. 800 m from the city. Regular connections with Milan (1 hr -1 hr 30 mins) - www.trenitalia.com.

MONEY

Cash – ATMs are everywhere in Milan but less common in smaller towns and rare in rural areas. Withdraw what you need before leaving the city.
Changing money –You can change money at banks, post offices and currency exchange counters. Commission is always charged.
Credit cards – Most hotels and upscale restaurants accept credit cards. Inexpensive bars and restaurants, especially at guest houses, are usually cash-only.

SEASONS AND CLIMATE

Temperatures in **Milan** in the spring vary from 16 °C to 22 °C. In the summer, the maximum temperatures, often reached in July, range from 25 to 35 °C. In the fall, temperatures remain high in September (21-26 °C) but start to fall in November (8-13 °C). In the winter, due to the humidity, even the highest temperature (approx. 5 °C) can feel pretty unpleasant. ♿ www.meteoam.it (Italian-language website).
The **lakes region** has a very pleasant climate all year round.
Late spring and early fall are the best times to visit the lakes region. In the winter, the cold and often humid climate can be off-putting and in summer the huge influx of tourists to the lakes can be a nuisance.

FIND OUT MORE

Tourist offices
Milan – Galleria Vittorio Emanuele II, angle Piazza della Scala - ✆ 02 88 45 55 55 - www.turismo.milano.it - 9am-7pm (w/end 6pm).
Bergamo – Torre di Gombito - Via Gombito, 13 - ✆ 035 24 22 26 - www.visitbergamo.net - 9am-5pm.
Lake Maggiore and Lake Orta – Addresses at www.distrettolaghi.it/fr.
Lake Como – Addresses at www.lakecomo.com.
Lake Garda –Addresses at www.visitgarda.com.

Websites
www.italia.it/fr: official website for tourism in Italy.
www.turismo.milano.it: tourism site for the city and province of Milan.

Emergency numbers
All-Europe emergency number: ✆ 112.
Mobile app: 112 Where Are U (App Store, Google Play and Microsoft Store)
Lost & found: ✆ 06 67 69 32 14.
Lost bank cards: Amex: ✆ + 33 (0)1 47 77 72 00, Master Card: ✆ 800 870 866, Visa: ✆ 800 819 014.

Basic information

USEFUL ADDRESSES

US Consulate – Via Principe Amedeo, 2/10 - Mon.-Fri. 8:30am - 12.30pm - ☎ 02 29 03 51 (24/7) - it.usembassy. gov/embassy-consulates/milan.
Consulate of Canada – Piazza Cavour, 3 -Mon-Fri. 9am-1pm ☎02 62 69 42 38 - www.canadainternational.gc.ca.
British Consulate – Via S. Paolo, 7 -Mon-Fri, 9:30am-12:30pm, 2-4pm. ☎ 02 723001 - www. gov.uk/world/organisations/ british-consulate-general-milan.

Bakery on Corso Garibaldi

© Opla/iStockphoto.com

COUNTERFEIT GOODS

Any person caught buying a souvenir that is a counterfeit product risks having to pay a fine of up to 10 000 €.

ELECTRICITY

Voltage across Italy is European standard, 220-230V. Plugs are types F and L (two or three round pins).

OPENING HOURS

Banks – Mon.-Fri. 8:30am-1:30pm, 2:30pm-4:30pm, sometimes open on Saturdays. Don't forget to take a numbered ticket on arrival.
Post offices – Mon.-Fri. 8:30am-1:30pm, Sat. 8:30am-11:50am. Some offices are open till 7pm. For more info, visit www.poste.it.
Churches – These are generally open from 8/8:30 am to 12:30pm / 1pm and from 4:30/5pm to 7/7:30pm. Some of them are closed in the afternoon.
Shops – The shops are generally open between 3pm and 7pm on Mondays, and from 10am to 7:30pm on Tuesday to Saturday. On Sundays, some grocery stores are open till 1pm and the most tourist-friendly shops in the downtown area are generally open all day.
Museums and sites – These are open between at least 10am and 5pm, sometimes until 6/7:30pm for the

most important ones. Last admission is generally 30 mins or 1 hr before closing time. Monday is the most common closing day.

Pharmacies – Look for the sign *farmacie* - and a green cross. They are generally open Monday to Saturday, from 8:30am to 12:30pm and from 3pm to 7pm; some are open 24 hrs. The names of the on-call doctors and the pharmacies that are open in the evenings and on Sundays are displayed. See also the website www.farmacieaperte.it.

INTERNET

All hotels offer free Wi-Fi. In Milan, the Free public Wi-Fi network covers a number of streets and public squares. See info.openwifimilano.it.

PUBLIC HOLIDAYS

🕭 The term for a public holiday is giorno festivo, while a working day is called a giorno feriale.
1 January – New Year's Day.
6 January – Epiphany.
Easter Sunday and Monday.
25 April – Anniversary of the country's liberation in 1945.
1 May – Labor Day.
2 June – Festival of the Republic.
15 August – Feast of the Assumption (*Ferragosto*).
1 November – All Saints' Day.
7 December – Feast of St. Ambrose, patron saint of Milan (*Sant'Ambrogio*).
8 December – Feast of the Immaculate Conception.
25 and 26 December – Christmas and St. Stephen's Day.

SAFETY

Milan is a relatively safe place, but as in any other big city, be wary of **pickpockets**, particularly in the busiest places (on public transportation, in the big stores, etc.).

MUSEUMS AND MONUMENTS

👌 *Opening hours, previous page.*
The admission prices are fairly high (from 5 € to 10/12 € for the major tourist attractions).
The national museums are free for under-18s and on the 1st Sunday of the month. Check the details at the ticket desk before you buy a ticket. Organized groups can usually get special rates for admission and the option of different opening times, by prior arrangement.
On the Night of the museums (Notte dei Musei) and in Cultural legacy week (Settimana dei Beni Culturali), the dates of which differ from one year to the next, some public institutions open their doors to the public free of charge.

POSTAL SERVICES

Stamps (*francobolli*) can be purchased at post offices and tobacconists. For a letter weighing > 20g, expect to pay 0.95 € for Europe, with the letter arriving in 4 to 5 days or 2,20 € for North America, with the letter arriving in around 14 days. The **mailboxes** are red.
Posta Centrale – Via Cordusio, 4 - 𝄢 02 72 48 25 08 (*open 8:20am - 7pm Sat. 8:30am -12:35pm - closed

Sun). For all information, check the website www.poste.it.

NEWSPAPERS

The daily Milanese newspapers with a national circulation are **Il Corriere della Sera** (*www.corriere.it*) and the daily financial paper **Il Sole 24 Ore** (*www.ilsole24ore.com*). Sports fans will enjoy **La Gazzetta dello Sport** (*www.gazzetta.it*).

You will also find the Milanese edition of the Roman daily La Repubblica (www.repubblica.it) and Il Giornale, which is owned by the Berlusconi family (*www.ilgiornale.it*). For movie theater listings and information about plays, concerts and exhibitions in Milan, check out ViviMilano, a supplement included with Il Corriere della Sera on Wednesdays, or its website: vivimilano.corriere.it.

At tourist offices or on the web (www.turismo.milano.it), you can also find Milanomese, a monthly publication offering insights into the main events taking place that month and practical information about the city's museums.

RESTAURANTS

Opening hours – Lunch is served between 12:30pm and 3pm and dinner is served between 7:30/8pm and 11pm. Many restaurants are closed on Sundays. Please note that some establishments may close over the summer. On Friday and Saturday nights, reservations are mandatory.
The check – Bread and the cover charge *(pane e coperto)* are generally added to the check (2-6 € depending

on the establishment). Service is usually included, too; if it is not, you will find the percentage (approx. 10%) indicated on the menu. No-one will demand a tip, but it is customary to leave a few euros after a good meal. At bars and concession stands you usually pay for what you're going to have at the cash register first, then take your ticket (scontrino) to the counter to place your order.

With the exception of concession stands and small stalls, **bank cards** are generally accepted everywhere.
On the go – Those on a tight budget can enjoy a *pizza al taglio* (by the slice) or a *panino*, either plain or *ripieno* (filled). The **paninoteca** (sandwich bar) offers a huge assortment of *panini*. Another option is to take advantage of the **aperitivo** (a 'happy hour' for the Milanese): for a fixed price (8-15 €), between 6pm and 9pm you can enjoy a drink and a few visits to a buffet offering charcuterie, raw vegetables and other appetizers.

SMOKING

Smoking is banned in all public places, restaurants, bars and nightclubs in Italy. The smoking ban also applies at hotels; some establishments offer rooms for smokers, however.

PHONE CALLS

Calls to Italy: 00 + 39 + no. of the call recipient, with the first zero included for land-line numbers and left out for cell phones. Cell phone numbers start with a 3.

Calls inside the country:
Within Milan itself, key in 02 +
no. of call recipient. To other cities,
key in the city code, always starting
with 0 + no. of the call recipient.

TRANSPORTATION IN MILAN

Public transportation
Milan's bus, tram and subway network
is managed by ATM (www.atm-mi.it).
You can buy tickets at subway
stations, tobacconists, newsstands
and cafés. Each ticket (1.50 €) is
valid for 90 mins (for a single journey
on the subway). 24-hr or 48-hr
tickets (valid from the time they are
validated) cost 4.50 € or 8.25 €.
The buses and trams operate between
5:30am and 1am, and the 4 subway
lines are in operation between
6am and 12:30am. Some tram and
trolleybus lines run all through the night.
The ATM Milano app lets you buy
tickets directly from your smartphone,
and you must then validate them
using the QR code scanners located
at subway entrances or on buses.

Sightseeing buses
City sightseeing Milano – www.
milano.city-sightseeing.it. Three
90-minute routes, with commentary
in several languages. Line A (historical
line) explores the downtown area
between the Piazza Duomo, Sforza
Castle and the Navigli; line B (modern
line) takes you from the northeast
of the city to the Stazione Centrale;
and line C (sport line) explores the
northern section of Parco Sempione,
as far as the Stadio San Siro and the
hippodrome.

The buses leave from Piazza Castello
and details can be found online.

Taxis
𝒫 02 85 85 - www.028585.it - app:
INTAXI; 𝒫 02 40 40 - taxiblu.it -
app: TaxiMilano ; 𝒫 02 69 69 -
www.026969.it - app: IT Taxi.
The taxis in Milan are white. There
are fixed rates for Malpensa airport
(90 €) and for trips between
Malpensa and Linate airports (100 €).
For Linate, the price is calculated by
the kilometer. Uber runs in Italy but
only in Milan. An alternative is MyTaxi.

Bicycles
All over Milan you will see the yellow
bicycles of **BikeMi** (both traditional
and electric). The charge is 4.50 €/
day, which includes 30min for the
traditional bikes; after that, you'll pay
0.50 €/30min.
The electric bikes cost almost twice
as much to hire. Max. usage is 2 hours
at a time. 𝒫 02 48 607 607 -
www.bikemi.com.

Cars
Driving – From Monday to Friday
(7:30am-7:30pm, 6pm Thursdays),
the Cerchia dei bastioni becomes
'**Area C'**: you can only enter this zone
if you purchase a ticket (5 €) that is
valid for the whole day and can be
bought at kiosks, tobacconists, ATMs
and parking meters, from a call center
(𝒫 800 437 437) or at www.comune.
milano.it). Access to the area must be
paid for by midnight of the following
day. Info: 𝒫 02 02 02.
Parking – Throughout almost the
entire city, parking is regulated
and a charge applies. The yellow

127

lines indicate spaces reserved for residents, while the blue ones indicate a paid parking space; pay at the time-stamp machine (with coins or a bank card). Parking in the city center is expensive: 3 €/hr for the first 2 hours and 4.50 €/hr for each hour after that (after 7pm, you only need to pay for the first 2 hours). Parking is free between midnight and 8am.

Recommended parking lot – San Barnaba parking lot, Via San Barnaba, a 10-minute walk from the Duomo (2 €/hr, 2 hr minimum, 1€/hr after the 6th hour of parking).

If **your car is towed**, contact the municipal police: 19, Piazza Beccaria - ☎ 02 77 27 02 80.

TRANSPORTATION IN THE LAKES REGION

You can buy a ticket that lets you travel all over the lakes region, valid for one day. There are night-time crossings in summer. *www. navigazionelaghi.it*.

Discover the region's untamed natural beauty on the **Lago Maggiore Express**, which travels between Italy and Switzerland by boat and train. *www.lagomaggioreexpress.com* - 34 €/24hrs, 44 €/48hrs.

SIGHTSEEING

VisitMilano is the free, official app for exploring the city: buy tickets straight from the app and get the latest information about what's on.

Tourist passes

The **3 Giorni Card - Tourist MuseumCard** gives you 3 days' free access to the municipal museums (Acquario, Castello Sforzesco, Galleria d'Arte Moderna, Museo Archeologico, Museo del Novecento, Museo delle Culture, Palazzo Morando, Museo di Storia Naturale and Museo del Risorgimento. Buy tickets at https://partnershop.ticketone.it/spl-civicimilano/#/ or at the ticket offices in the museums - 12 €.

The MilanPass includes reductions, a free pass for all public transport in the city, or the City sightseeing Milano (*see p. 129*), and free access to several museums, including: the terraces and museum at the Duomo, the theater museum at La Scala, the Pinacoteca di Brera, Gallerie d'Italia, Triennale Museum, Museo della Scienza and Museo della Tecnologia. On sale at Zani Viaggi - Milan Visitor Center, Largo Cairoli/Via Cusani - ☎ 02 86 71 31 - www.themilanpass.com - 69 €/48hrs.

The **Case Museo Card**, valid for 6 months, gives you admission to the Bagatti Valsecchi and Villa Necchi Campiglio, and to the Poldi-Pezzoli museum. ☎ 02 45 47 38 00 - www.casemuseomilano.it - 20 €.

The **Abbonamento Musei Lombardia Milano** card gives you access to almost all the museums in Milan, Bergamo, Como and the lakes of Lombardy. ☎ 02 89 70 90 22 - lombardia.abbonamentomusei.it - 45 €/1 yr.

Festivals and events

ANNUAL EVENTS

January
▶ **Corteo dei Magi** – (6 Jan.)
Procession of the Magi at Epiphany:
a costumed street parade from the
Duomo to Sant'Eustorgio.

▶ **Fashion Week** – The mens' fashion
collections for the autumn and winter
season are unveiled in late January,
while the ladies' collections are
unveiled in late February; as for the
spring collections, they come out
in late June for the men, and late
September for the ladies.

February
▶ **Capodanno cinese** (*Chinese New
Year*) – Shows, concerts and costume
parades on the Via Paolo Sarpi, in the
heart of Milan's Chinatown.

February/March
▶ **Carnaval Ambrosiano** – (Sat. after
Ash Wednesday) The longest carnival
in Italy, with a huge parade.

March/April
▶ **Tempo di Libri** – International
publishing conference. www.tempo
dilibri.it/it
▶ **International furnishings
conference and Design Week** –
(mid-Apr.) This event transforms the
city's galleries, bars and restaurants
into bustling forums for exuberant
discussion of all things design.
salonemilano.it et www.fuorisalone.it.
▶ **Marathon Stramilano** – Tens of
thousands of runners take to the city's
streets. www.stramilano.it.

▶ **MiArt** (Fiera internazionale d'arte
moderna e contemporanea) – For all
those with a passion for modern and
contemporary art. www.miart.it.

▶ **Festival pianistico internazionale
di Bergamo e Brescia** – (late April to
mid-June) A prestigious international
piano festival, hosted jointly by the
Donizetti theater in Bergamo and
the Teatro Grande in Brescia.
www.festivalpianistico.it.

May
▶ **Cortili Aperti** – For one Sunday only,
the most attractive palace courtyards
in Milan are opened up to the public,
free of charge.
www.adsi.it, section 'Giornate ADSI '.
▶ **Pianocity Milano** – For three days,
the city's public and private spaces
play host to hundreds of piano
concerts and recitals.
www.pianocitymilano.it.

June
▶ **Festa dei Navigli** – (1st Sun.)
Festivals, processions and concerts
along the length of the Navigli.
Illuminations at night.
▶ **Milanesiana** – A multi-disciplinary
festival, featuring concerts, plays,
exhibitions and cultural shows.
www.lamilanesiana.eu.

July/August
▶ **Settimane musicali** – Symphonic
music at Stresa and at other
locations near Lake Maggiore.
www.stresafestival.eu.

September

▶**MiTo Settembre Musica** –
Between Milan and Turin, jazz, world music, classical music and avant-garde music.
www.mitosettembremusica.it.

November

▶**Bookcity Milano** – A huge 4-day festival dedicated to books, with multiple events throughout the city.
http://bookcitymilano.it.

December

▶**Artigiano in Fiera** – For one week, enjoy a unique opportunity to meet some of the world's greatest arts and crafts experts and admire their creations: traditional souvenirs, fabrics, food, fashion. http://artigianoinfiera.it.
▶**Prima della Scala** – (7 Dec.) The Festival of St. Ambrose, patron saint of Milan. A gala evening to mark the opening of the Milanese opera season.
www.teatroallascala.org.

ART GALLERIES

Galleria Artesanterasmo – *Via Sansovino, 5 - ⓜ Lima ou Piola - ℘ 02 87 70 69 - www.artesanterasmo.it - 9:30am-1pm, 2pm-6pm - w/end by appt. A historic name in the Milanese art scene, specializing in the great Italian artists such as Salvatore Fiume.*
Galleria Blanchaert – *Piazza Sant'Ambrogio, 1 - ⓜ Sant'Ambrogio - ℘ 02 86 45 17 00 - www.galleria blanchaert.it. Founded in 1957, this gallery exhibits contemporary decorative artworks.*
Galleria Blu – *Via Senato, 18 - ⓜ Montenapoleone - ℘ 02 76 02 24 04 - www.galleriablu.com - 10am-12:30pm, 3:30pm-7pm - closed w/ends. Founded in 1957, Galleria Blu offers visitors a panorama of post-war Italian art and works by up-and-coming Italian artists.*
Galleria Cardi – *Via Marco de Marchi, 2 - ⓜ Turati - ℘ 02 49 47 30 64 - www.galleriacardi.com. Some of the great names of the Italian trans-avant-garde and international artists.*
Anna Maria Consadori – *Via Brera, 2 - ⓜ Montenapoleone - ℘ 02 72 02 17 67 - www.galleriaconsadori.com.* Italian art and design from the 1930s onwards.
Monica De Cardenas – *Via Francesco Viganò, 4 - ⓜ Garibaldi - ℘ 02 29 01 00 68 - www.monicadecardenas.com.* Works by up-and-coming and renowned artists.
Galleria Massimo De Carlo - MDC – *Via Ventura, 5 - ⓜ Lambrate - ℘ 02 70 00 39 87 - www.massimodecarlo.it - 11am-7pm - closed Sun. Great names from the contemporary scene in a spectacular setting.*
Galleria Antonia Jannone – *Corso Garibaldi, 125 - ⓜ Moscova - ℘ 02 29 00 29 30 - www.antoniajannone.it - 3:30pm-7:30pm - closed Sun. and Mon. Founded in 1976, this gallery celebrates architecture in all its forms: designs, mock-ups, sketches, prints, etc.*
Kaufmann Repetto – *Via di Porta Tenaglia, 7 - ⓜ Moscova - ℘ 02 72 09 43 31 - www.kaufmannrepetto.com - 11am-7:30pm - closed Sun. and Mon.* Œuvres d'artistes milanais plus ou moins célèbres.

131

Find Out More

133

Installation for Milano Design Week - Fuori Salone - at Pinacoteca di Brera
© Nicola Marfisi/AGF/age fotostock

Milan: a timeline

6-4 BCE – The territory of Lombardy is inhabited by the celtic tribes of the Insubres.

49 BCE Milan becomes a Roman municipality; it is the main city in Cisalpine Gaul.

222-196 BCE – The Insubres are forced to cede their territory to the Romans.

286-402 – Thanks to its importance and its position, Milan becomes the capital of the Western Roman Empire.

313 – Constantin promulgue l'édit de Milan, qui accorde aux chrétiens la liberté de culte.

374-397 – St. Ambrose (339-397) is Bishop of Milan.

452 – Attila the Hun sacks the city.

490 – Theodoric the Great and his Ostrogoths take control of the Po Valley.

539 – Milan is razed to the ground by the Ostrogoths.

568-774 – The Lombards establish a kingdom with Pavia as its capital.

11-12 C – Milan is governed by the Archbishops.

1155 – Emperor Frederick Barbarossa is crowned King of Italy.

1167 – Milan founds the **Lombard League** with the neighboring cities to oppose Frederick Barbarossa.

1176 – Victory in the **Battle of Legnano** against Barbarossa. With the Peace of Constance (1183), the Lombard territories obtain administrative autonomy.

1278 – **Otton Visconti** (1207-1295), Archbishop of Milan, becomes Lord of the city.

1386 – The Visconti family initiates the construction of the Duomo.

1395 – Gian Galeazzo Visconti (1351-1402) becomes Duke of Milan.

1447 – **François Sforza**, the son-in-law of Filippo Maria, the last of the Viscontis, takes power in Milan and, in 1454, is proclaimed Duke.

1494-1499 – Ludovico Maria Sforza, known as **the Moor** (1452-1508) turns Milan into a new Athens by enticing some of the great minds of the age to the city.

1482-1500 – **Leonardo da Vinci** works in Milan for Ludovico Sforza.

1499-1500 – The French king Louis XII attempts to conquer the city. Ludovico is captured and taken to France, where he spends his final years at the Château de Loches.

1521-1525 – Battle between France and Spain for the Duchy of Milan.

1535-1713 – Spanish rule.

1538-1584 – **San Carlo Borromeo** is Archbishop of Milan.

1564-1631 – **Federico Borromeo** is Archbishop of Milan.

1630 – Milan is ravaged by an epidemic of the plague, as described by Manzoni in *The Betrothed*.

1706 – Milan is occupied by the Habsburgs.

1713 – Under the Peace of Utrecht, Milan is given to Austria.

1778 – Inauguration of the opera-house La Scala with the opera Europa riconosciuta (Europa revealed) by Antonio Salieri.

1797 – Milan becomes the capital of Napoleon's Cisalpine Republic.

1805 – Milan becomes the capital of the Kingdom of Italy and Napoleon is crowned in the cathedral.
1815 – After the fall of Napoleon, with the Congress of Vienna, Lombardy is handed back to Austria. Milan is the capital of the Lombardo-Venetian Kingdom.
18-22 March 1848 – During the **Five Days of Milan**, the city revolts against the Austrians, in the context of the First Italian War of Independence.
1859 – During the Second War of Independence, Austria is defeated by France. On 8 June 1859, the Austrians abandon Milan: Napoleon III and Vittorio Emanuele II of Savoy enter the city in triumph.
1900 – Assassination of King Umberto Ist in Monza by the anarchist Gaetano Bresci.
1919 – Benito Mussolini founds the **Fasci di Combattimento** in Milan, the nucleus of what will go on to become the National Fascist Party.
1925 – Inauguration of the Milano-Laghi motorway, one of the first in the world.
13-16 August 1943 – Milan is bombed by the Allies: 2 000 people are killed and 23% of the city is turned to rubble. The Galleria Vittorio Emanuele, the Duomo, the Palazzo Reale, and the church of Santa Maria delle Grazie are all badly damaged. In September, the **Italian Social Republic** is born in Salò, on Lake Garda.
24 April 1945 – Insurrection of Milan against Nazi occupation.
On 28 April, Mussolini is shot at Giulino di Mezzegra, on Lake Como.

1958 – Milan metro opens first line.
1958 – Milan Fashion Week is established.
12 December 1969 – The attack at Piazza Fontana (16 people killed) marks the start of armed political unrest and the Years of Lead.
1990 – Department store 10 Corso Como opens; it will go on to open in Seoul, Shanghai, Beijing, and New York.
1992 – Start of the so-called **Mani Pulite** ('clean hands') judicial investigations which send shock-waves through the Italian political system.
1994 – The Milanese entrepreneur **Silvio Berlusconi**, owner of AC Milan and founder of the Mediaset group, wins the general election.
2012 – Death of Carlo Maria Martini, the much-loved Archbishop of Milan from 1979 to 2002.
April 2015 – Inauguration of the port of Milan (the Darsena), after it is closed for several years.
May-October 2015 – Universal Exhibition with the theme *'Feeding the planet, energy for life'*.
June 2016 – Giuseppe (Beppe) Sala, backed by the Democratic Party, is elected mayor of the city.
December 2017 – Inauguration of the CityLife Shopping District, one of Italy's biggest urban shopping centers, to complete the re-purposing of the former Fiera di Milano district.

135

Great moments in Milan's history

THE HEART OF THE WESTERN EMPIRE

Milan is thought to have been Gaulish territory originally, but in 222 BC the Romans took the town, and it was they who were at the origins of its development. It went from being a humble village to a full-scale Roman city, with a forum, numerous temples and other public buildings. At the end of the 3rd century AD, Emperor Maximian made it the capital of the Western Roman Empire. The city's population is around 150,000 at this time. In 313, Constantine publishes the **Edict of Milan**, which grants Christians freedom of religion.

FROM THE LOMBARD KINGDOM TO THE GHIBELLINES

In the 5th and 6th centuries the region was beset by Babarian invasions, before the Lombards founded a kingdom here with Pavia as its capital. Pavia was conquered in 756 by Pepin the Short, King of the Franks, whose son Charlemagne seized the Iron Crown of Lombardy, the symbol of Italian royalty. In the 12th century, to fight off the German emperor Frederick Barbarossa, who wished to take control of the region, Milan forms the Lombard League (1167) with its neighboring cities and wins the **Battle of Legnano**, thereby safeguarding its autonomy. In the 13th century, the **Visconti** family takes power. Its most famous member, **Gian Galeazzo** (1351-1402), skilled soldier and man of letters, assassin and devout believer, becomes Duke of Milan (1395) and has the cathedral and the Certosa di Pavia built. His daughter Valentina marries the grandfather of Louis XII. This union will eventually lead to the rows over inheritance that prompted the Italian Wars.

A bishop before he was even baptized

Ambrose (339-397), an imperial governor born in Trier, is one of the most notable characters from the Roman Empire: he was the man who restored a climate of peace among Milan's Christians, who were divided over Arianism; he was so well-liked that he was elected bishop by popular demand, before he had even been baptized. He updated the liturgy and the Milanese church's calendar of feast days, which to this day conforms with the Ambrosian rite. He is celebrated on 7 December.

THE ARRIVAL OF THE SFORZAS

In 1447, following the death of Filippo Maria, the last member of the Visconti family, Francesco Sforza, his son-in-law and *condottiero*, leads the **Sforza** family to power. Its most illustrious member, **Ludovico il Moro** (1452-1508), turns Milan into a new Athens by luring the greatest minds of the age here, including Leonardo Da Vinci and Bramante. Louis XII proclaims himself to be the true heir to the Duchy of Milan, however, and attempts to conquer it in 1500. Francis Ist follows suit, but is defeated by the determined troops of Charles V in the Battle of Pavia.

FROM SPAIN TO THE KINGDOM OF ITALY

From 1535 to 1713, Milan is ruled by the Spanish. In this period, two figures leave their mark on the city in a religious and humanitarian sense: **Carlo Borromeo** (1538-1584; canonized in 1610) and **Federico Borromeo** (1564-1631), charitable defenders of the city during the plagues that ravage it (1576 and 1630).

Under Napoleon, Milan is the capital of the Cisalpine Republic (1797) and the Kingdom of Italy (1805).

After being regained by the Kingdom of Italy, the city becomes a major player in the economic, financial and cultural life of the country and a metropolis renowned throughout Europe.

AMBITIOUS PROJECTS IN THE 21ST CENTURY

The city is currently experiencing profound architectural change, as it seeks to re-purpose certain areas and express its economic vitality through ambitious architectural projects. Among the refurbishment projects, besides the Palazzo Lombardia and the Museo del Novecento, is the new **FieraMilano Rho**, construction of which was launched by the architect Massimiliano Fuksas, and the renovation of La Scala and the Stazione Centrale. At the site of the former Fiera, the **CityLife** complex, by the architects Hadid, Isozaki and Libeskind, features luxury homes, daring skyscrapers and dedicated spaces for culture and leisure. In the Garibaldi-Repubblica district, the **Porta Nuova** project, designed by twenty international architects, changed the area's profile by incorporating towers, green spaces, arts centers, offices and businesses. South of Milan, on Lake Isarco, the new **Fondazione Prada** complex (Rem Koolhaas, OMA) has appeared, while in the square XXIV Maggio, at the confluence of the two Navigli, the **Darsena**, Milan's historic port, is being regenerated.

Art and architecture

THE MIDDLE AGES AND THE RENAISSANCE

From the sober Roman style to the return of classical art

In its essence and in the history of its art, Milan is a 'Roman city' thanks to the extraordinary basilicas founded by St. Ambrose. **Lombard Roman art**, which emerged in Lombardy in the 10th century, is characterized by sober and harmonious lines, a solid and massive structure, a gable roof, thin vertical strips or 'lesenes' on the façade, light arcades with semi-circular arches and a layout generally featuring three naves, covered with crossed vaults, and with three apses, with solid round pilasters on the inside. One of the examples that best represents this style of architecture is Milan's Basilica Sant'Ambrogio (*see p. 46*). The beauty of the Lombard Roman-style churches also owes much to the stone carvers.

The **Gothic** style, which arises in France in the middle of the 12th century, only reaches Italy a century later. Its great emphasis on the vertical and its flying buttresses fail to seduce the Italians, used as they are to the Roman forms, and windows are few and far between, so as to allow room for frescoes. In Milan, the enormous Duomo, with its buttresses, its 3200 statues and 135 spires built into the roof and façade, mark the high watermark of a uniquely flamboyant Gothic style in Italy.

In the **Renaissance**, the most acclaimed architects are Florentin Michelozzo (1396-1472), **Filarete** (1400-1469), who builds one tower of the Castello Sforzesco and the Ospedale Maggiore, and above all **Donato Bramante** (1444-1514), the favorite master of Ludovico il Moro. An admirer of antiquity and the imagination, he invents façades composed of alternating bays, pilasters and niches which confer a sense of harmony on so many Renaissance buildings. Bramante begins his career in Milan (Santa Maria presso San Satiro, the Basilica of Sant'Ambrogio) and Pavia, but achieves his greatest feat with the designs for the reconstruction of St. Peter's basilica in Rome.

Painting

In painting, the Lombard school puts the search for 'beauty and grace' above all else: its most celebrated exponents are Vincenzo Foppa (1427-1515), Bergognone (1450-1523) and Bramantino (between 1450 and 1465-1536). The works of the painters Andrea Solario (around 1473-1520), **le Sodoma** (1477-1549) and above all the delicate works of **Bernardino Luini** (circa 1480-1532) attest to the decisive influence of **Leonardo da Vinci** (1452-1519), who is staying in the city. Da Vinci is a man of astonishingly diverse talents: architect, painter,

A city of waterways

The network of defensive canals that once surrounded the city was also an active communication system, making it possible to link the waters of the Ticino with those of the Adda. The Naviglio Grande, created in the 12th century to defend Milan from Pavia, an ally of the German Emperor Barbarossa, soon became a navigable waterway that was used to transport – among other things – the marble required for the construction of the Duomo. The canals – with the exception of the Naviglio Grande and the Naviglio Pavese – were covered over in the 1930s. The Naviglio Martesana is only visible today in the Via Padova area (north east of the city center), and the mark left by it can be seen on the Incoronata sluice (a dual-lock system that Leonardo da Vinci helped design), between Via San Marco and Via Castelfidardo (see map on p. 30). Since 1819, the Naviglio Pavese has been connected to the Ticino thanks to a series of sluices.

sculptor, mathematician. Having trained in Florence under Verrocchio, Leonardo spends many years in Milan, where he paints *The Last Supper* on the walls of the convent of Santa Maria delle Grazie between 1495 and 1499. Among other things, he is the inventor of *sfumato* (from the Italian word for 'smoky'), the hazy effect obtained by superimposing layers of extremely delicate paint on one another, giving shapes imprecise outlines. Already influenced by the Lombard Caravaggio and Baroque art, the Milanese **Arcimboldo** (1527-1593) brings a new twist to the still life by making portraits out of fruit, vegetables, flowers and fish.

THE CATHOLIC REFORMS

Two archbishops from the Borromeo family play a fundamental role in Milan's artistic development in the 16th and 17th centuries: **Carlo Borromeo** (1538-1584), present at the Council of Trent, supports the Catholic Reforms and helps the Milanese during the plague epidemic of 1576,

and his cousin **Federico** (1564-1631), founder of the Biblioteca Ambrosiana. At their instigation, painters decorate the churches of Milan: Giovanni Battista Crespi, known as **Cerano** (1573-1632), **Giulio Cesare Procaccini** (1574-1625), **Morazzone** (1573-1625), **Daniele Crespi** (circa 1598-1630). In the same era, the architect **Pellegrino Tibaldi** (1527-1596) is very active, working for Carlo Borromeo.

18TH AND 19TH CENTURIES

In around 1750, there is a return to Greco-Roman forms. This neoclassicism is successfully exploited all over the peninsula by the Venetian **Antonio Canova** (1757-1821), whose sculptures pay homage to classical art. In Milan, the most important exponent of Neo-Clacissism is **Giuseppe Piermarini** (1734-1808), the architect of La Scala, one of the most important opera-houses in the world. The eclectic nature of the second half of the century owes its greatest project, the **Galleria Vittorio Emanuele II**, to **Giuseppe Mengoni**

(1829-1877), who dies after falling from the roof of the gallery, days before it is inaugurated.

In the late 19th century, the **Liberty** style prevails, a style affiliated to Art nouveau, then in vogue in Europe. It adds to the elegance of the residential areas populated by the Milanese bourgeoisie, around the Castello and along Corso Venezia. The Lombard **Giuseppe Sommaruga** (1867-1917) creates a number of buildings with abundant floral decorations, such as the **Palazzo Castiglioni** on Corso Venezia (see *p. 24*).

THE 20TH CENTURY

The capital of futurism

The poet **Filippo Tommaso Marinetti** (1876-1944) publishes the *Manifesto of futurism* in the French daily *Le Figaro,* in 1909. It was in Milan, though, that futurism found fertile ground. Marinetti, who splits his time between Paris and Milan, declares all-out war on tradition, and this futurist current sings the praises of modernity, symbolized by the industrial city - a riot of speed, machines, light, noise, crush and energy. These ideas will be picked up on by the painters **Umberto Boccioni** (1882-1916), **Giacomo Balla** (1871-1958), **Gino Severini** (1883-1966), **Carlo Carrà** (1881-1966) and the architect **Sant'Elia** (1888-1916). Their works attempt to translate the dynamism of the modern world through fragmented forms that are related to the language of cubism; what sets them apart, though, is their sense of movement and the violent,

excitable disorder that is present, whose origins are expressionist. These artists' ambition is to spread futurism to every aspect of daily life: architecture, music, theater, cinema, furniture, clothes, cooking and advertising.

The major movements of the 20th century

After the Great War, the general climate of a 'restoring of order' affects many Italian artists. In 1922 the **Novecento** group is formed in Milan at the initiative of seven artists, including **Mario Sironi** (1885-1961) and **Achille Funi** (1890-1972). Margherita Sarfatti, an art critic (known for having been close to Mussolini), is tasked with coordinating the movement. The Novecento develops the foundations of naturalism, filtered through a re-reading of medieval and classical Italian art, with results that are often very poetic, displaying remarkable formal concentration. Most Italian painters, sculptors and architects adhere to this attitude or are at the very least influenced by it, particularly when the Fascist regime declares itself to be in favor of this stylistic trend in the 1920s. A counter-movement forms, with some of the most vibrant forces in Italian art of the day grouped around the representatives of the Milanese **Corrente** school, the **Roman school** and the **Turin Six** who, despite following their own separate paths, are all interested in expressionist solutions.

These artists often arrive at an intensely tragic realism, great social tension and profound human

141

substance. Among the most notable sculptors is the Bergamese **Giacomo Manzù** (1908-1991), who updated the forms of Christian art. His profound feel for light, which imparts a Donatello-esque vitality on his sculpture and on his bas-reliefs in particular, enables him to denounce violence, perceived as the mortification of the human being.

The post-war years

Following the tragedy of the Second World War, there is talk of 'the death of art': artistic expression adopts new approaches, including a disavowal of the traditional physical medium of the canvas. This is to some extent the case with **Alberto Burri** (1915-1995): in making collages on old, damaged canvases, he is not attempting to represent something, but to expose a fragment of material that acquires meaning thanks to the artist's intervention. **Lucio Fontana** (1899-1968), born in Argentina, completes his apprenticeship at the Accademia di Brera, in Milan. He tears at, punches holes in and lacerates the canvas, as he seeks new solutions to the old problem of space, which can be created but not represented. He thereby underlines the importance of the 'gesture', the action that brings what's on this side of the canvas into contact with what's beyond it, and destroys the classic method of staging space.
Piero Manzoni (1933-1963) seeks the infinite by working on *Achromes* (colorless paintings), but his most celebrated (and shocking) work is *Artist's shit in tin cans*.

142

ARCHITECTURE IN THE 20TH AND 21ST CENTURIES

In the early 20th century, **Como** is a center of modern architecture thanks to **Giuseppe Terragni** (1904-1943)and **Antonio Sant'Elia** (1888-1916), skilled proponents of a rationalism that espoused a 'no-frills' construction style, liberated from a past that was now academic.
Pier Luigi Nervi (1891-1979) also has a role to play in modern architecture. A Lombard, adept at working with reinforced concrete, he creates masterpieces that combine strength, simplicity and elegance: Milan's Pirelli Tower (1959), built in collaboration with the Milanese **Gio Ponti** (1891-1979), is a blend of rationalism and classical tradition.
Renzo Piano (born in Genoa in 1937), the star behind the Centre Pompidou in Paris, designed the Milan head office of the newspaper *Il Sole 24 Ore* in Via Monte Rosa. The works of **Gae Aulenti** (1927-2012), who trained at Milan's school of architecture, include the renovation of the Piazza Cadorna. **Vittorio Gregotti** (born in 1927) is the architect behind the Teatro degli Arcimboldi and the Bicocca district, while **Massimiliano Fuksas** (born in 1944) created the FieraMilano Rho in 1944 *(see p. 139)*. **Stefano Boeri** (born in 1956) helped shape the contemporary urban landscape: his Bosco Verticale skyscraper, erected in the Porta Nuova district *(see p. 51)*, won the International Highrise Award in 2014.

Design

If fashion found its theater in Milan (*see p. 146*), design paved the way for it in the early days of the 20th century. In the 1930s, the architects and designers of the Rationalist movement **Giuseppe Terragni** (1904-1943) and **Franco Albini** (1905-1977) strove to counteract Neo-Classicism inspired by the French Art Deco movement. Italian design truly took off at the start of the 1950s. Born in Milan in 1891, **Gio Ponti**, painter, architect and industrial designer, directed Milan's Triennale of art and architecture and founded the **Domus** review. A promoter of rationalism in architecture, he played a considerable role in the rebirth of Italian design in the post-war period. His chair *Superleggera*, designed for Cassina in 1955, won the Golden Compass design award. **Joe Colombo** (1930-1971), **Achille** (1918-2002) and **Pier Giacomo Castiglioni** (1913-1968) also contributed to the enormous vitality of their field.

In 1976, **Alessandro Guerriero** (born in 1943) establishes Studio Alchimia, which shifts towards playful design inspired by **Alessandro Mendini** (born in 1931). Before joining Alchimia, **Ettore Sottsass** (1917-2007) designs several products for Olivetti that achieve fame, like the first Italian computer (*Elea 9003)* and the bright-red portable typewriter *Valentine* (1969). Sottsass leaves

Alchimia in 1981 to form **Memphis** and revive radical design. Up until 1988, he produces furniture, ceramics and textiles with eccentric and colorful patterns, which will play a decisive role in internationalizing post-modernism.

Vico Magistretti (1920-2006) creates works that celebrate the simplicity of forms: his creations feature in MoMA's permanent collections in New York. Founded in Milan in 1949, the **Kartell** group specializes in making plastic products (household utensils designed by Gino Colombini, furniture, etc.). Ten years later, another Milanese firm, **Artemide**, starts producing furniture and lights that helped to cement the reputation of Italian design.

Milan plays host to schools (like the **Scuola di Design** at the Politecnico di Milan or the **IED, Istituto Europeo di Design**), showrooms and an **International furniture conference**, in April, which is the cornerstone of all this design activity. While the main conference takes place at the FieraMilano Rho complex, the fascinating exhibitions and demonstrations of the **Fuori Salone** (Milano Design Week), are focused mainly around **Via Tortona**, in **Brera** and in the workshops and art galleries of **Via Ventura**, in the outlying district of Lambrate. These events turn the city into the global capital of design for a week.

A capital of fashion

As you'll soon realise after spending a few days in Milan, good taste and elegance are what the city is all about. It should come as no surprise, then, that along with New York, Paris and London, it hosts one of the four most important weeks in fashion in the world. During the **Milano Fashion Weeks**, held twice a year in February-March and September-October, the city becomes a theater for fashion shows and photo-shoots. In the heart of the city, linked by an imaginary red carpet, the spaces of the **Fashion Hub** project which host the fashion shows come to life: the Palazzo Giureconsulti (*Via Mercanti, 2*), the Circolo Filologico (*Via Clerici, 10*), the Palazzo Clerici (*Via Clerici, 5*) and the Piazza d'Armi at Castello Sforzesco. The other key locations during Milan's fashion weeks are in the Solari district (⚲ *see p. 45*).

The **Superstudio Più** (*Via Tortona, 27*) is a new venue for major events and fashion shows, and incorporates several photographic studios. Lastly, at no. 59, Via Borgognone is the headquarters of Armani and the **Teatro Armani**, designed in a minimalist style by Japanese architect Tadao Ando and used as the setting for Armani's own shows.

Milan can lay claim to having been the birthplace of the greatest names in fashion. The pure creativity of **Giorgio Armani** is expressed in his garments: inventive and classic at the same time, and always impeccable.

The offbeat **Dolce & Gabbana** are the inventors of an ironic, trendy look, with a false carelessness and a deliberate flamboyance. **Gianfranco Ferré** puts the emphasis on "quality and comfort"; **Prada** is known for the classic and rigorous lines of its collections, for which the quirky fabrics and prints, and the accessories, provide an extravagant counterpoint; **Trussardi** favors simple lines and flawless tailoring and finishes; in a word, luxury in its most sober form. The **Versace** fashion house, lastly, offers a rich and sumptuous style, adored by rock-stars.

The sisters **Carla** and **Franca Sozzani** are among the most influential figures in the fashion world. Carla, the elder of the two, runs a gallery and is the founder of the *concept store* **10 Corso Como**, a temple of Milanese fashion; Franca, a journalist, was editor-in-chief of the Italian edition of *Vogue* magazine from 1988 until her death in 2016, at the age of 66.

Some of the most notable younger designers are Anna Francesca Ceccon (*www.moimultiple.com*), Mauro Gasperi (*www.maurogasperi.com*), Chicca Lualdi (*www.chiccalualdi.it*), Francesca Liberatore (*www.francescaliberatore.eu*) and Andrea Turchi (*www.andreaturchi.com*).

Literature and publishing

In the Enlightenment age, Milan is at the center of Italian culture, thanks to figures like **Cesare Beccaria** (1738-1794), author of the treatise *On crimes and punishments* (1764), an extraordinary little book in which the intellectual explores issues that are still very topical today, such as the death penalty. A romantic author par excellence, **Ugo Foscolo** (1778-1827) spends the most creative years of his career in Milan. His most famous work is the ode *The Sepulchers* (1807). The Milanese **Alessandro Manzoni** (1785-1873) is the author of the historical novel *The Betrothed* (1827), set in the 17th century between Lake Como, Milan and Bergamo, under the Spanish occupation.

A hundred years after Manzoni, another great Milanese writer makes his mark on history: **Carlo Emilio Gadda** (1893-1973). By setting out to deform the language, Gadda rebels against fascism and bourgeois stupidity. He shares with the French author Céline a fondness for slang, onomatopoeia, neologisms and dialects. **Giorgio Manganelli**

(1922-1990) also goes against the realist tradition, so as to give free rein to his fertile imagination.

Giovanni Testori (1923-1993) is one of the greatest Catholic Italian playwrights of the 20th century. In poetry, there is **Giovanni Raboni** (1932-2004), author of a landmark translation of Proust's *À la recherche du temps perdu,* and **Alda Merini** (1931-2009), who sought with an intense and painful voice to express the human condition. In 1997, the Nobel Prize in Literature is awarded to the Milanese actor and playwright **Dario Fo** (1926-2016). Fo, the most widely performed playwright in the world, adopted the tradition of farce and political theater, using Grammelot, an invented language based on a mish-mash of onomatopoeia and words, supplemented with mimes.

The detective novel – the *giallo* (yellow), after the series with yellow covers by the publisher Mondadori – comes to the fore, thanks to **Giorgio Scerbanenco** (1911-1969) and **Andrea G. Pinketts** (born in 1961).

The home of Italian publishing

A number of publishing houses are headquartered in Milan. Feltrinelli, founded in 1954, became famous with its very first title, an autobiography of Nehru. In 1949, Rizzoli launched its Biblioteca Universale Rizzoli (BUR), the first collection of literary masterpieces at affordable prices. Oscar Mondadori's paperbacks are among the bestsellers at newsstands. Milan is also home to the country's biggest daily newspaper, Il Corriere della Sera, and the most important financial newspaper, Il Sole 24 Ore.

Theater and cinema

STAGE

Milan is home to one of the world's most prestigious stages. Opera house La Scala *(see p. 18)* has hosted great classical musicians like Milan's very own **Maurizio Pollini** (born in 1942), the outstanding violonist **Uto Ughi** (born in 1944) and Milanese conductor **Claudio Abbado** (1933-2014).

Variety music found an outlet in the work of Lombard singer-songwriters like **Enzo Jannacci** (1935-2013), **Giorgio Gaber** (1939-2003), who combined theater and song, and **Adriano Celentano** (born in 1932), an actor known for his *one man shows,* and a singer who has sold over 70 million records. **Moni Ovadia,** a Milanese of Bulgarian descent (born in 1946) is the outstanding performer of Jewish theater and music, above all Yiddish songs. In keeping with a tradition dating back to the Sforzas (in the late 18th century), Northern Italy remains a prestigious area for the practice and teaching of **dance**. After the war, the Milanese ballerina **Carla Fracci** (born in 1936) achieves worldwide acclaim with her interpretations of romantic roles (*Juliet* and *Gisèle*) alongside Rudolf Noureïev. The Piedmontese **Roberto Bolle**, whose talent was spotted by Nureyev, is promoted to principal dancer at La Scala in 1996; since 2003 he has been its étoile dancer.

SCREEN

After the war, the abandoning of the cinema of propaganda and evasion from the 1930s-1940s leads to the birth of **Neo-Realism**, which seeks a return to the specific, an attentive observation of the human and social realities of everyday life. The Milanese **Luchino Visconti** (1906-1976) lays the foundations for this movement with *Ossessione* with its natural-looking set, in 1943. In its slipstream came the Lombards **Alberto Lattuada** (*Our War*, 1945) and **Luigi Comencini** (*Hey Boy*, 1948). Neo-Realism faded away in the 1950s, as it was no longer in step with the desires of a public longing to move on from the years of misery. **Dino Risi** (1916-2008) then made a number of farcical comedies, the most famous of which are *The Easy Life* (1962), *I Mostri* (1963) and *Scent of a woman* (1975).

In the 1960s-1970s, while Visconti expands his oeuvre with *Rocco and his brothers* (1960), **Marco Ferreri** (1928-1997) a turbulent iconoclast, launches an assault on modern ways with *Dillinger is dead* (1969) and *La Grande Bouffe* (1973).

In 2003, **Marco Tullio Giordana** enjoys considerable success with *The Best of Youth*, a six-hour series made for TV, which relates the tale of the country's last three decades through the story of one family.

147

Food and drink

Let's start with a few basics: the word for breakfast is *colazione*, lunch is *pranzo*, and dinner is *cena*.

THE DIFFERENT COURSES

Antipasti (starters)

The most common one in Milan is cured meat, *sottaceti* (vegetables in vinegar), *carpaccio*, and marinated sardines or anchovies. *Bresaola* is a type of dried beef from the Valtellina, a valley in the alps that comes out at the northern end of Lake Como.

Primi piatti (first course)

Generally one of the many, many different varieties of pasta. There are four main pasta families. **Dry pasta**: *spaghetti, tagliatelle, penne, tagliolini, maccheroni, linguine, farfalle, bucatini...*, which are boiled and served with a sauce or a meat *ragù*. Then there is **stuffed pasta**: *ravioli, agnolini, tortelloni* et *cappelletti*. Stuffed with meat, cheese or vegetables, they are served with or without an accompanying sauce or in a bouillon. In addition to these two main categories there is also **fresh pasta**, which can be flavored with herbs, served with tomato, or prepared with special flour, such as *pizzoccheri della Valtellina* (made with buckwheat flour), and a vegetable accompaniment. Finally there is also **oven-baked pasta** served with a meat sauce, vegetables or cheese. The best-known varieties are *lasagne* and *cannelloni*.

The Piedmontese part of the Po Valley, which produces a large amount of rice, is the land of **risotti**, delicious dishes of rice cooked in a bouillon and served in an infinite number of ways. The most famous are served with saffron, ceps *(porcini)* or white or black truffles. **Polenta**, cooked using maize flour, is a dish that originated among peasant communities in the alpine regions. It is a traditional *primo*; occasionally it accompanies meat dishes and cured meats. **Gnocchi** are made from potatoes and served as a starter.

Secondi piatti (second/main course)

If you're still hungry after your pasta, you can tuck into the main course: a dish of meat or fish and vegetables. Veal is usually served in a breaded cutlet (schnitzel), known as '**Milanese style**'. There is also **ossobuco**, veal knuckle with tomato, with an accompaniment of *riso allo zafferano*. Beef is served raw in a **carpaccio**, or cooked as tournedos and strangely known as **stracotto d'asina** – literally 'donkey stew'. A popular main course in Northern Italy is **bollito misto**, assorted boiled meats with complementary sauces.

148

Contorno

This is the garnish for the *secondo piatto*: it is never pasta, but instead boiled or, very often, grilled vegetables. The *contorno* must be chosen when you place your order and will often be served on a separate plate.

Formaggio (Cheese course)

Northern Italy is a wonderful region for cheeses; the specialties of Lombardy are *gorgonzola*, *provolone*, *quartirolo* with spring-time milk and various types of *stracchino*, a soft cheese made with cow's milk.

Dolce (dessert)

There's an extensive selection of desserts, starting with the famous *tiramisù*. Be sure to try *crostata* (a fruit tart), *panna cotta* (cooked cream usually served with a red fruit coulis), *affogato al caffè* (vanilla ice cream drizzled with hot coffee), *budino al cioccolato* (chocolate flan) and *zabaione*. *Panettone* is a brioche loaf with candied fruit and raisins, served at Christmas. A *semifreddo* is a cold dessert, and ice cream (*gelati*) is, of course, one of the great Italian specialties, as are sorbets.

Caffè (coffee)

If you just order a coffee, you'll be served an *espresso*. It is almost always *ristretto* (strong) and you may find it surprisingly intense. The *caffè lungo* (long coffee) is espresso with more water, so it's toned down. For the equivalent of a filter coffee, ask for a *caffè americano*. The *cappuccino* is a coffee with frothy milk on top (Italians only drink a *cappuccino* at breakfast-time), and the *macchiato* is coffee with a dash of milk. If you'd like a little alcoholic beverage to go with your coffee—sometimes be poured straight into the cup—ask for a *corretto*.

STILL OR SPARKLING?

The Italians adore their sparkling wines, which can be white or red. in **Franciacorta**, near Lake Iseo, all manner of sparkling white or rosé wines are produced.
Also excellent are the red wines of the **Valtelina**, near Switzerland, and those of the **Oltrepo Pavese**, around Pavia.

A GOURMET FESTIVAL

The brainchild of journalist Paolo Marchi, the festival **Identità Golose** (*www.identitagolose.it*) held in late January or early February in Milan, has been bringing together the 'creme de la creme' of contemporary cooking and pastry-making since 2005. Each year, a different region of Italy and country are highlighted, through their chefs and their specialties.
This festival takes the form of large demonstrations where each chef provides his recipes for one particular product, technique or cooking style. You can also enjoy the best of Italian foods, presented by the people who produced them.

149

INDEX

150

154

Photo credits

Page 4
Duomo: © Luciano Mortula/iStockphoto.com
Sforza Castle: © Maurizio Borgese/hemis.fr
Novecento Museum: © justhavealook/iStockphoto.com
The Last Supper: © Image Asset Management/age fotostock
Basilica di Sant'Ambrogio: © marcociannarel/iStockphoto.com

Page 5
Pinacoteca di Brera: © C. Labonne/Michelin
San Lorenzo Maggiore: © M. Marca/Michelin
The Borromean Islands: © LucaLorenzelli/iStockphoto.com
Bergamo: © Karol Kozlowski/iStockphoto.com
Bellagio: © Roberto Moiola/age fotostock

Maps

Inside
Duomo to Castello Sforzesco *p17*
Quadrilatero della Moda and Corso
    Venezia *p25*
Brera and Corso Garibaldi *p30*
Pinacoteca Ambrosiana and
    Old Milan *p33*
Ca' Granda and Ancient Canals *p38*
Porta Ticinese, Navigli and Solari *p44*
Corso Magenta & Sant'Ambrogio *p48*
Bergamo *p60*
Lake Maggiore and Lake d'Orta *p67*
Lake Como *p76*

Cover
Lombardy & the Lake Region
    Inside front cover
Milan's districts
    Inside back cover

THEGREENGUIDE short-stays **Milan Bergamo & the Lakes**

Editorial Director	Cynthia Ochterbeck
Editor	Sophie Friedman
Production Manager	Natasha George
Cartography	Peter Wrenn, Theodor Cepraga
Picture Editor	Yoshimi Kanazawa
Interior Design	Laurent Muller
Layout	Natasha George

Contact Us

Michelin Travel and Lifestyle North America
One Parkway South
Greenville, SC 29615
USA
travel.lifestyle@us.michelin.com

Michelin Travel Partner
Hannay House
39 Clarendon Road
Watford, Herts WD17 1JA
UK
℘01923 205240
travelpubsales@uk.michelin.com
www.viamichelin.co.uk

Special Sales

For information regarding bulk sales,
customized editions and premium sales,
please contact us at:
travel.lifestyle@us.michelin.com

MICHELIN

travelguide.michelin.com
www.viamichelin.com

short-stays

- ◆ Charleston
- ◆ London
- ◆ Milan Bergamo & the Lakes
- ◆ New Orleans
- ◆ New York
- ◆ Paris
- ◆ Reykjavik

159

Visit your preferred bookseller for the short-stay series, plus Michelin's comprehensive range of Green Guides, maps, and famous red-cover Hotel and Restaurant guides.

Michelin Travel Partner

Société par actions simplifiées au capital de 15 044 940 EUR
27 cours de l'Ile Seguin - 92100 Boulogne Billancourt (France)
R.C.S. Nanterre 433 677 721

© Michelin Travel Partner
ISBN 978-2-067239-94-4
Printed: January 2019
Printer: Estimprim